Saving "Rocky Horror" From Orphan To Icon

By
Tim Deegan

(SP)

Published by Sutton Press, Los Angeles

ISBN # 979-8-9989931-0-7

Table of Contents

Dedication

For Laddie

When nobody else would listen to me,

he said "go ahead and try it".

Acknowledgements

Only two men believed in me and what I wanted to do with "The Rocky Horror Picture Show" once it was judged by Fox to be a bonafide failure and sent to the depths of the studio's vaults.

One was Alan Ladd, Jr. (popularly known as "Laddie"), the studio head at 20th Century Fox that gave me the green light to take "Rocky Horror" to midnight, after my bosses fired me, twice, for attempting to take what was considered a failed movie off the shelf.

Laddie had never seen the movie, knew what it was about, or met Lou Adler. He only asked me one question which was how much I expected the midnight shows to gross. I went out on a limb and said $5 million. He didn't blink...all he said was "go ahead and try it". He was betting on me, not the movie.

Success has many stepfathers (only failure is an orphan). Laddie was the quiet man behind the scenes--the stepfather who was not afraid to take a risk or believe in a person's passion like he did with me and "Rocky Horror".

Fans may never have heard his name, but should know that he was the critical link--the green light-- between obsolescence for "Rocky Horror" and the enjoyment for so many passionate fans for the past 50 years.

How critical this man was to linking my dreams with what has become a reality for so many fans is why I have dedicated this book to him.

The other "believer" was Executive Producer Lou Adler. He knew I was operating all alone at Fox, without any studio support, until Laddie stepped in. He gave me constant support and encouragement to follow my dream.

Over the past five years, I exchanged 568 emails with Lou for fact checking, clarifications of questions, and for feedback. It was more efficient than speaking with him, and gave me instant documentation and, where necessary, verification of facts.

It was reassuring that, a half century later, his memory of events practically always matched mine, and he occasionally gave me something that I didn't know. Similarly, I revealed a few things to Lou that I had never told him before about my struggle to get "The Rocky Horror Picture Show" taken off the shelf at Fox and sent to a midnight release.

Lou was very generous with his time and his brain, and I am grateful for that. And, 99% of the time he replied to my email inquiries within minutes. Nothing lingered. He matched my tempo beat for beat.

This book tells a story about the bigger mid-century context that Lou and "The Rocky Horror Picture Show" fit into. There's some of what I call "new scholarship" about Lou Adler in these pages that may serve as a primary source for his eventual biographer.

Lou Adler was always supportive and encouraging as I wrote this book, telling me, as he read galleys: "It is going to be a very well written and informative book, Tim". (10/15/20).

I hope readers agree.

Tim Deegan

Los Angeles, CA

2025

Chapter 1
My Introduction to "Rocky Horror"

Adopting a movie that had become an orphan.

It was anything but love at first sight for me and the movie "The Rocky Horror Picture Show." There was a double negative: I didn't like the movie, and my studio bosses didn't like what I wanted to do with it.

In fact, when producer Lou Adler asked me what I thought of the movie, I told him that I didn't like it, even though my job as a marketing executive at 20th Century Fox was to support every movie on the release schedule, regardless of how I felt personally about the movie.

But, my relationship with the movie about "Sweet Transvestites From Transexual Transylvania" slowly morphed into action as I saw both of us shunned and disregarded by Twentieth Century Fox, two underdogs: one a man and the other was a movie.

No studio had ever played a movie at midnight, so I had no precedent to refer to for support of my thesis that "The Rocky Horror Picture Show" should be played in theaters at midnight, after it failed at its first run at the box office. I had personal experience going to midnight movies with my friends, and instinctively felt that "Rocky Horror" could find a home in the late night darkness. All I had was my gut instincts, eventually some trickery, and lots of persistence that grew even more passionate with the resistance I faced from the studio. I spent a lot of time and energy fighting the studio to make them understand my goal of releasing "The Rocky Horror Picture Show" at midnight.

I place "Rocky Horror" in several contexts in this never before told true story of "how 'The Rocky Horror Picture Show' happened" and how it was saved. From the beginning, it benefited from the support of a fierce fan base, becoming the longest continuously running movie in history since its first midnight show on April 2, 1976.

One context is the late 1960's and early 1970's just ahead of the 1975 release of the movie. It was a time when two dramatic ruptures happened in Hollywood. The original moguls that built the movie business from scratch were phasing out and being replaced by corporate ownership of movie studios.

Simultaneously, the public taste in movies was rejecting the "old" Hollywood that was still presenting them with movies like "The Sound of Music" (1965) and shifting their interests to the "new" Hollywood producing movies like "Bonnie and Clyde" (1967). The name that society gave this revolution was "counterculture," and Hollywood was desperate to give the counterculture movies they wanted to see.

While the shift in control of movie studios and picture selection were two important contextual settings for the daring "Rocky Horror Picture Show" (1975), other contexts were just as important as what was happening in an underground LGBTQ+ community, and what was happening with established music producer turned "Rocky Horror Picture Show" executive producer Lou Adler.

"Rocky Horror," is also necessarily a story about Lou Adler. My personal experience with him began when "Rocky Horror" was a stage play at his Sunset Strip nightclub, The Roxy and I was one of the Fox executives in the audience. I was with my colleagues (Peter Myers the general sales manager, Jonas Rosenfeld, the head of marketing, Publicity Director Johnny Friedkin, Advertising Director

Steve Panama, and me, Advertising Manager) who were being asked by the studio's president if Fox should acquire the movie rights to the play. Our collective and unanimous decision was "no," when we met in Roxy's driveway after the show.

It was overturned by the studio president Gordon Stulberg only after he laid off some of the costs and risks (and sacrificed potential profits) in a financial deal that has been kept secret for a half-century until now.

Adler was attempting to create a new construct for himself as a rare Hollywood hyphenate: music mogul and movie maker.

In the nineteen-fifties, Lou imprinted Jan & Dean on the pop culture consciousness. It was what he called "Surf music and culture, with the tall blond California look," as opposed to "Philadelphia's Italian of Frankie Avalon, Bobby Rydell, and Fabian," that had been prominent then. (1)

Placing himself at turning points of counterculture pop history in the sixties, Lou Adler continued to make big impacts on the music scene in California: the "Monterey International Pop Music Festival" "The Mamas and the Papas," the romantic ballads of Carole King, and the stoner comedy of "Cheech and Chong." He was burning the California vibe deeper into pop culture. Now, in the early seventies, Lou was ready to put his stamp on Hollywood with a daring and avant-garde movie about "Sweet Transvestites From Transexual Transylvania."

There was a symbiotic relationship between Lou Adler and "Rocky Horror Picture Show,": without him, it would not have been produced, and without its success, his eventual movie career may not have made such a rebound from the failure of Robert Altman's "Brewster McCloud," (MGM-1970) which Lou produced.

Underpinning all that would follow was the person who would become "The Rocky Horror Picture Show," 'godmother': Britt Ekland. She was dating Lou, and he was on his way to London to see their infant son Nicholai, when Ekland told Adler about the stage play she just saw and encouraged him to go see it ASAP. After seeing the play, Lou quickly made a deal with British Impresario Michael White, the play's producer, to bring the play to America and eventually make a movie version of it.

This book is about "history"—movie history, some new scholarship about Lou Adler, "Rocky Horror," and the Fan Club, the cyber community and shadow cast's history, all told by the people that made that history.

My struggle, as a very young Fox executive, was to take this shelved movie into release as a midnight show in the pop culture milieu of the early 70s when music, movies, movie studios, the LGBT+ community, politics, youth, etc, were all going through a very transgressive period.

"Success has many stepfathers—only failure is an orphan"— is a Hollywood truism that applies whenever a hit movie emerges. Many people wind up trying to take credit when the box office is big. There were, however, several legitimate "stepfathers" (and one "godmother") that made "The Rocky Horror Picture Show," success possible, from the inception of the story through the decades-long run at midnight.

Legendary MGM studio production head and "Boy Wonder," Irving Thalberg (circa early 1900's), once said, "If it weren't for the writing, we'd have nothing. Writers are the most important people in Hollywood, and we must never let them know it" (2) There would be no "Rocky Horror" without writer and creator Richard O'Brien, who wrote the original story, the screenplay, and the song lyrics.

Tim Curry created the indelible signature role of Dr. Frank 'N Furter and played it both on the stage and the screen.

Producer Michael White stepped in as the original impresario to stage the play in London and briefly shared producer status with Lou Adler. Additionally, had Britt Ekland not encouraged her boyfriend Adler to see the stage play in London "Rocky Horror," it may have been an asterisk, not a phenomenon.

A quartet of Twentieth Century Fox executives Gordon Stulberg, Alan Ladd, Jr, Robert Sherman, and myself were the inside men at Fox that paved the way for the movie version of the play and its theatrical distribution.

Two of these men, Stulberg and Ladd, were successive Fox studio presidents. Sherman led the negotiations, Stulberg acquired the movie, and Ladd, who succeeded Stulberg as studio head. He gave me the green light to go to -midnight. At that time I was a young twenty-something marketing novice.

Without Bill Quigley, the head booker for the Walter Reade Organization, who heard my pitch and signed up for the first midnight show at The Waverly, "Rocky Horror," may never have seen midnight. And once the movie was playing at midnight, Sal Piro stepped forward and became the Founder and President of the "The Rocky Horror Picture Show" Fan Club. Everyone in this small group played a key role in launching and sustaining the culture this movie facilitated.

Notes

1. to author 4/20/19

2. https://www.azquotes.com/author/31313-Irving_Thalberg)

Chapter 2
Meet the Godmother of "Rocky Horror"

A movie star encourages her boyfriend to take a look at the "Rocky Horror Show" stage play. He does, he buys the rights, and makes the movie.

Abraham Lincoln upon meeting Harriett Beecher Stowe, the author of "Uncle Tom's Cabin", said ""So this is the little lady who started this Great War." (1) One could ask Swedish actress Britt Ekland the same question about "The Rocky Horror Show". Like Stowe, Ekland could say "yes", because she was the instigator of bringing Richard O'Brien's creation, and impresario Michael White, to the attention of her then-boyfriend Lou Adler.

Like the creation of life, the "Rocky Horror Picture Show" phenomenon begins with a mom or, more appropriately, a godmother. Britt Ekland is known to a generation of film fans as the "Bond Girl" Mary Goodnight, in the James Bond film "The Man with the Golden Gun" (1974).

As Britt recalled it, she "first saw 'The Rocky Horror Show' at the Classic Cinema on Kings Road [in]… early fall 1973". At the time, she knew her boyfriend was "looking for something special to put into The Roxy Theatre in LA" where Lou was part owner. She followed her instinct that this show would be perfect with its "ingenious" music, and "perfect" performances. She recalls that, "it is very seldom [one] get[s] the feeling of having been part of something so totally new and revolutionary" as Rocky Horror has proved to be.

When she called Lou to London they "attended a party given by Hercules Belleville [and] Lou was introduced to 'The Rocky Horror Show' producer Michael White...[they] started the conversations

6

that would lead to an agreement that would bring 'The Rocky Horror Show' to the Roxy". And as time has shown, Lou "came, he saw and the rest is history!" (2)

It was only six months between the club's opening and the play's premiere. Lou was booking The Roxy with musical acts, but a long running edgy and avant-garde musical play with a gloss of sexuality for every taste, could be a club-booker's dream.

Lou was celebrating the grand opening of The Roxy, his Sunset Strip nightclub, on September 23, 1973 with a three-night performance by Neil Young (who, decades later would become his brother-in-law) and planned on premiering "The Rocky Horror Show" there, which he did less than six months later on March 24, 1974.

Eventually, it had a nine-month long run and was the start of what would become the "Rocky Horror" industry of movies, music, merchandising and licensing that has lasted for five decades, with no letup in sight.

It was at Lou's Stone Canyon mansion, near the Bel Air Hotel, that I saw how connected Lou and Britt were. A housekeeper met me at the door and showed me into the living room, where Lou introduced me to Nicholai, his then-very young son. Britt was due to call shortly, Lou explained as he showed me the auction catalog picture of the antique Lalique crystal ashtray they were planning to bid on from a Paris auction in a few days.

Lou had been reading "Nicholas and Alexandria", Robert K. Massie's biography of the last Tsar and royal family of Russia and the fall of Imperial Russia, when he named their son Nicholai. (3) Now, a half-century later, Nicholai co-owns The Roxy, where "The Rocky Horror Show" made its Southern California debut.

Britt and Nicholai share a second familial stream with Lou that goes beyond shared DNA; it's the dripping blood bond with "Rocky Horror". It was Britt, the unheralded 'godmother', who was the spark to the light that was shined upon "Rocky Horror" for Lou to see. Nicholai, as both he and the movie pass the half-century mark, may find himself bringing symmetry to what his mom started by being sure that "There's (always) a Light (Over at the Frankenstein Place)". (4) His mom discovered it, his dad nurtured it and, hopefully, he can be the spiritual son to keep lighting the anniversary candles.

Notes:

1. https://www.csmonitor.com/Books/chapter-and-verse/ 2011/0630/The-little-woman-behind-a-very-big-war

2. Adler as agent for Ekland to author 2/22/19

3. to author 11/23/18

4. Composers Richard O'Brien and Richard Hartley, Lyrics Richard O'Brien

Chapter 3
A Crosscurrent of Circumstances

How a fifteen-year accumulation of random decisions led me to be the architect of the midnight show release.

There might never have been hundreds of thousands of fans for "The Rocky Horror Picture Show" or a movie that has played continuously for fifty years, without a flow of criss-crossing circumstances in my life that I had practically no control over.

These included a boating accident, corporate proxy fights for control of a railroad and a movie studio, an urgent telegram, a movie studio owner looking for a better deal in Las Vegas, and being a "tag-along" to a meeting with a producer.

These circumstances cumulatively led to how I wound up at Fox and was put in a position where I would eventually rescue "The Rocky Horror Picture Show," (1975) from the studio graveyard, and turn it into a midnight show phenomenon that has made it the longest continuously running movie (now 50 years and counting) in history.

The chances of me ever meeting Lou Adler, or having anything in common with him, or saving his movie were zero. I knew who he was because I liked his music, mostly Carole King and The Mamas and the Papas. Even when we both were at Metro-Goldwyn-Mayer, where I was a young international division executive, and he was the producer of Robert Altman's "Brewster McCloud" (1970) there was no proximity. I saw him physically on the studio lot a few times at a distance, but that was it.

For me, as a teen and a young twenty-something, the excitement of being at MGM was Stanley Kubrick ("2001: A Space Odyssey"), Michelangelo Antonioni ("Blow Up," and "Zabriskie Point,") and David Lean ("Doctor Zhivago," and "Ryan's Daughter." Those were the unique experiences, including being an intern for Kubrick on "2001" that made working in a movie studio meaningful for me. These men were the "Mount Rushmore" of movie directors at MGM in the late sixties and very early seventies. Adler was a music guy wanting to be a movie maker in an environment where practically everyone wanted to be a movie maker.

Our paths did not cross until we were both at Fox in the early 70's. Again, I was a studio executive, and Lou was the producer of "The Rocky Horror Picture Show." An unlikely series of circumstances led to this intersection of me and Lou Adler. Once we were both at Fox, and with the movie's arrival for release, the rest became history.

My getting there actually began several years earlier, when I was an adolescent who would hear a harrowing story from an older sister. A young boy in a sailboat, she told me, suffered a blow to the head when the boom swung across the boat as it was making a turn, and the boy did not duck in time to avoid being hit in the head. Consequently, he was knocked down and maybe out, and possibly overboard, and could have even drowned. A ten-year-old's imagination connected all those imaginary dots, and I was immediately traumatized by the prospect of attending sailing classes that summer. It was one thing, as I heard from an older brother who already sailed (as did my older sister and my mom), that they tested you by making you jump into the water fully clothed to see if you could stay afloat with all your clothes on for several minutes replicating your boat capsizing and a rescue craft being on the way to pull you out of the water. But, to possibly die in a sailing accident, as my imagination suggested, was far more than I expected from summer camp. I needed an alternative.

My mom stepped in to solve my anxiety by suggesting to my dad that he take me to his office each morning to be an office boy, which he did after I tried one summer of sailing. It got me into the habit of working summers in an office environment and eventually led to a summer internship at MGM. The sailing drama launched by my big sister began the criss-cross of circumstances that led me to "The Rocky Horror Picture Show."

When I was born, my dad was a vice president of the Chesapeake & Ohio Railroad, and on the team that helped the C&O's owner, Robert Young, acquire control, through a proxy fight, of the New York Central System, like the C&O, one of the country's great railroads.

Someone who was skilled in winning a corporate proxy fight was just what Robert O'Brien, the CEO of Metro-Goldwyn-Mayer, was looking for because a MGM board member had launched a proxy fight to take control of the studio. The spoils of that proxy fight victory for my dad included obtaining a summer job at MGM for one of my older brothers, but he wanted to sail that summer, so he asked me if I wanted to fill in for him.

As an adolescent, I had moved from being a Deegan Company assistant to the office boy at its midtown Manhattan office for a few summers to a downtown job as a clerk in the corporate secretary's office at the American News Corporation, running errands to Wall Street. All I wanted was to be back in midtown at lunch hour, not at the mouth of the Holland Tunnel which is where American News was located. I gladly filled in the job at MGM for my brother that had it but wanted to sail instead.

I spent the next few teenage summers at MGM until they relocated the corporate headquarters to their Culver City, California production studio. I wanted to get away from the small New England town where I grew up and check out California, so I moved west myself thinking I could work for MGM again, but now as a full-time employee.

Based on my experience at MGM for three summers, I obtained a job as a co-op advertising clerk learning how studios and theaters co-operated to advertise and promote movies in every city, big and small. It also taught me the importance of grassroots promotion in smaller markets.

About a year later, I transferred to the International division as assistant to the Foreign Publicity Manager.

That executive, a Brit, soon returned to England, and his job was split in half: he took oversight of MGM's publicity operations in the UK, Europe, the Mid-East, and East and South Africa. At age 23, I was promoted to Foreign Publicity Manager with oversight of Latin America, Australia and New Zealand, and what was called the Far East, which then consisted of Japan, Hong Kong, Singapore and Malaysia, and Taiwan. MGM had branches in all these territories and every other major global market.

I was kept very busy learning about international trade, import and export, and local publicity and media options in every country in my remit. My foreign department colleagues and I also screened movies almost daily for acquisition by MGM International distribution. The MGM International distribution apparatus, then the strongest in Hollywood, reached every foreign market, and included branch offices and sometimes MGM theater circuits.

The job also included travelling, first to Latin America, and then a planned trip to MGM's Tokyo regional headquarters and other stops in Asia to meet my MGM colleagues there. Traveling to Down Under would round out my territorial tour.

A fateful telegram hit my desk late on a Friday afternoon that changed everything. The world was not yet Marshall McLuhan's "global village" which resulted in the need for long paper trails to conduct business in foreign countries from MGM's world headquarters at the Culver City studio. The choice formats were circular letters (the same letter to all foreign branch offices), individual letters, and telexes and telegrams. Phones were rarely used.

Every morning, a pile of communications were distributed to each foreign department executive that consisted of both incoming and outgoing circulars and telegrams so we could all be up to date on the broad operational strokes of the foreign division.

I would never have seen a telegram that helped shift me from MGM to Fox if I was not in the foreign department's loop. One Friday afternoon, I received a call from someone I knew at an advertising agency that worked for both MGM and Twentieth Century Fox, who tipped me off that Fox was looking for a candidate to fill an advertising manager's job. He told them about me. While flattered, I was working on the itinerary for my Asia trip and declined the chance to meet the Fox executive until the man told me I had nothing to lose by meeting an executive from another studio interested in me, so I agreed to a breakfast meeting with the Fox executive the next morning at his home.

Knowing nothing about advertising but having a strength in publicity and international operations did not phase the guy. He needed help right away and offered what would be a big salary increase. Even with that, I declined, explaining that my priority was traveling to Asia for MGM International. As I neared my car, I suddenly remembered that the foreign department's communications batch from the day before included an urgent telegram from MGM president James Aubrey to the several regional managing directors of the international division to travel immediately to attend his press conference at MGM studios on

Monday morning. While I didn't know why, the fact that the studio president ordered top international executives to fly in from around the world seemed like something very big was about to be announced..

I spun around, knocked on the front door, and asked if it was too late to change my mind and accept his offer. He gladly said he'd love to have me at Fox. It turned out that Aubrey would announce that studio owner Kirk Kerkorian was closing MGM and relocating the MGM brand name to Las Vegas to apply to his gambling enterprises, and hotels, and even possibly anchoring offshore MGM gambling ships on the Pacific and Atlantic coasts. Almost all of my MGM colleagues lost their jobs with this decision.

At Fox, I was told all I needed to learn about advertising, and being the studio's advertising manager would come from practical hands-on experience interacting with the advertising agencies, and attending most team meetings with my bosses and the VP of advertising and publicity. I was told I was welcome to "tag-along" but to ask no questions if there was a producer in the room, until after the meeting.

Depending on my workflow, I had the option to attend or decline these meetings, but usually tried to make them. So, when I heard there would be a meeting with Lou Adler I marked my calendar to be sure to attend. I wanted to see him up close and suspected I might learn something from his unique perspective as a music, not a movie person. Music was a faster turning, more street-oriented business than movies, and Lou was all-street, with a strong track record of music successes. He would prove, as I worked with him on the release of "The Rocky Horror Picture Show", to be far more adept at connecting with audiences than the movie people.

Lou came to his introductory meeting with the advertising, publicity, and sales teams, and I kept silent, until he asked my opinion of his movie. I was the odd man out: ; everyone else was, falsely I knew, encouraging. I told him I didn't like his movie. He said he liked that objectivity, and asked that I be the only person to interact with him from Fox.

Any one of these circumstances, the boating accident, the proxy fights, filling in a job at MGM for my brother, moving to California, a fateful telegram, tagging along to meetings, telling Lou the truth may not have happened.

Even one missing from the sequence could have sent me on a different trajectory away from ever connecting with Lou Adler and "The Rocky Horror Picture Show".

Chapter 4
The Deep Down Under
Roots of "Rocky Horror"

Where it all began: Australia and New Zealand.

In the beginning, there was Australia and New Zealand. From the creative talents native to those two countries sprang a play called "The Rocky Horror Show" which became the movie "The Rocky Horror Picture Show".

Richard O'Brien, who wrote the original stage production's book, music, and lyrics and co-wrote the screenplay, based on the stage version, with Jim Sharman, was raised in New Zealand. Jim Sharman, the director and co-writer of the screenplay, and Brian Thomson, the designer, are both Australians, as is the film's editor, Graeme Clifford. Nell Campbell, who originally played Columbia, is also Australian.

Both countries have contributed richly to the "Rocky Horror," phenomenon.

Here are a few interviews that show how special "Down Under," is to "Rocky Horror.".

A third interview, with Australian Kristian Fletcher and "Cards 4 Sorrow," in Brisbane, Australia, is in the chapter called "Oh God, my dad's wearing fishnets and heels..." as are some vivid recollections and impacts by Australian Tony Pazuzu.

'"Rocky Horror' has always offered freedom, liberation, and fun." (1) An interview with Paige Foley of the Hot and Flustered Shadowcast, Auckland, New Zealand.

TD - How do you feel about the success of "Rocky Horror" in New Zealand?

PF - New Zealand is well-known for our homegrown legends that reach above and beyond expectations, which is certainly something that "Rocky Horror," has achieved! We try to take inspiration from this to create a show that is far beyond what you would expect from our scrappy amateur cast with just a can-do attitude, fishnets, and so much glitter.

TD - What do you think of having a statue of Richard O'Brien there?

PF - Embassy Park marks the birthplace of "Rocky Horror," and is home to the Riff Raff statue. In 2019, the cast was given the amazing opportunity to perform in the park for Richard O'Brien in celebration of the statue's 15th anniversary. It was such an honour for our cast to show our love for this crazy show and such an inspiration to hear his appreciation for all of our hard work.

TD - How did you get connected to "Rocky Horror?"?

PF - Like much of the cast, I was introduced to the show by my parents when I was far too young. If they had thought that would lead to me running around in public in my underwear, I'm sure they would have thought twice about it! The cast runs regular open casting calls for people of all levels of experience, ; the only requirement is a passion for "Rocky Horror.".

TD - How did "Hot and Flustered," get started as a shadow cast, and how long has it been performing?

PF - Hot and Flustered originally got started as Evil Deeds back in 2011 as an unofficial shadow cast. This group was encouraged to develop and grow by Stephanie White, who had previously been involved in a shadow cast in Berlin. Since its formation the cast has grown and developed in experience and ability.

TD - How has "Rocky Horror," impacted the cultural scene?

PF - "Rocky Horror" has always offered freedom, liberation, and fun. In the Hot and Flustered cast, we are driven by our desire for creating a fully inclusive environment where everyone can be themselves. As a group we have always been part of the LGBTQ+ community and are proud of the diverse family we have created. Over the years we have seen many of our cast build their confidence and pursue their passions in both drag and burlesque performances.

TD - Does the movie play regularly, or just special occasions?

PF - We perform every 3-4 months, often in celebration of a special event. The highlights of the year are our Pride and Halloween shows, as we mix up the casting and costuming to really make the show our own! With a fairly small but very devoted audience, we perform at our local heritage theatre on Friday evenings with all the classic cult fun, including virgin games, costume competitions and prop kits.

"It was great when it all began, and it still is." An interview with Mark Jabara. *(2)*

When the stage play "The Rocky Horror Show," was getting set to be filmed as the movie "The Rocky Horror Picture Show,", the producers needed a replacement for Tim Curry, who had played the Frank 'N Furter role in London and Los Angeles. Actor-singer Paul Jabara was chosen.

Paul's cousin, Mark Jabara, followed his cousin's career closely, and became a big fan of "Rocky Horror.". He recounts the Down Under "Rocky Horror," experience here.

TD - How did you get connected with "Rocky Horror?"?

MJ - My personal interest comes from my cousin Paul Jabara, who replaced Tim Curry as Frank at The Roxy in LA in 1974.

TD - Has "Rocky Horror" always been popular in Australia?

MJ - The show and film were, and are, huge in Australia. The show is currently playing again. "Rocky Horror," has been popular in Australia since 1974, when the show first opened.

TD - Can you tell me some of the backstory about Jim Sharman?

MJ - Australian Director, Jim Sharman, was only 24 when he was selected to design and direct the Original Australian cast of the American musical "Hair,", that opened in Sydney, June 4, 1969. A major success running for 2 years in Sydney, it transferred to Melbourne, on June 8, 1971, again directed by Sharman, but redesigned by Brian Thomson. The new set included a massive rainbow of lights that spanned the proscenium. Among the cast were Reg Livermore and Graham Matters, both would go on to feature in the original Australian run of "The Rocky Horror Show.".

Producer Harry M. Miller, who co-produced "Hair", followed it, in 1972, with "Jesus Christ Superstar", again directed by Jim Sharman and designed by Brian Thomson, with the title role played by Trevor White. The show was to be the springboard for the pair's foray into international recognition, when they were chosen to design and direct the 1972 Original London production.

TD - How did Paul Jabara get involved?

MJ - The London role of Herod was given to American actor, singer/songwriter, and my cousin, Paul Jabara, who'd been a cast member of the original Off-Broadway and Broadway casts of "Hair". His understudy was New Zealand-raised actor Richard O'Brien, and one of his back-up dancers was Perry Bedden.

TD - How did Richard O'Brien fit in?

MJ - During the first year of "Superstar", Richard O'Brien began speaking of an idea he was having about writing a rock musical of his own, with a sci-fi theme. At that point, he was calling it "It Came

From Denton High", and he'd play his guitar and sing the song "Science Fiction" to anyone who showed interest. Sharman and Thomson did show interest, as both had a passion for old science fiction films and had just completed an experimental film of their own, called "Shirley Thomson Versus The Aliens" (Shirley was played by Jane Harders, who'd later go on to play Australia's first Janet).

One night, Jabara took a night off, due to illness, and O'Brien's misguided Elvis-inspired interpretation of Herod wasn't well received, which saw Richard let go from the show. Despite this, he remained friends with Sharman and Thomson, during this era when many performers and creatives from Down Under were traveling to London, some for experience and others finding major success, like Barry Humphries, and Clive James.

TD - What about the creation of the "Little Nell" character?

MJ - One such performer was Laura Campbell, daughter of Sydney newspaper columnist Ross Campbell, who wrote stories about his family using character names from Charles Dickens in place of their real names. Laura was referred to as "Little Nell", which became her stage name. A friend of Sharman and Thomson, she would go on to fame through her association with them, with a role written especially for her in the show that was to make them all iconic.

TD - And Richard O'Brien kept moving forward?

MJ - Riding a wave of popularity, thanks to the huge success of their production of "Superstar", several productions followed and they often included Richard O'Brien. Richard had continued working on his musical, and when Sharman was offered The Royal Court Theatre to direct a show of his choice, he instead asked if he could have the tiny Upstairs Theatre, to workshop Richard O'Brien's musical concept. With financial and advertising backing by theatrical entrepreneur and producer Michael White, who'd been impressed by a set of songs O'Brien had recorded on a cassette, a limited season of rehearsal and performance was set in mid-1973.

TD - How did O'Brien and Sharman collaborate on the "Rocky Horror" script?

MJ - Richard O'Brien had no experience with script writing and relied heavily on Jim Sharman to put the ideas he had into a serviceable format. Sharman, Thomson, and O'Brien, pooled their resources, their love of kitsch, science fiction, rock n roll, and the grotesque, born of life in the lands of Australia and New Zealand, to fashion a show that Sharman named "The Rocky Horror Show.".

TD - What were some of the influences that you think may have helped shape the script?

MJ - In both the U.K. and Australia, suburban cinemas were coming down, a trend that had begun decades earlier in the USA, thanks to a loss of attendance brought about by television. In a bid to draw audiences back, two types of film had found prominence, "Carry On" comedies, a series of 21 frivolous, sexy, double-entendre-laden movies (O'Brien had done stunt work on one), and Hammer Studios horror movies, which had found success with colorful, sexually charged, remakes of America's old Universal monster classics. These movies dominated suburban cinemas in both Britain and Australia. "Rocky Horror" would become an homage to these films and their impact, in this period of destruction.

TD - What about Brian Thompson's design concept?

MJ - Brian Thomson conceived the idea of setting the show in a cinema under demolition, with a lone usherette reminiscing about the movie's of the past that had impressed her, before presenting her fantasy, in which she would take the role of the maid, with an

"American" couple from the black and white films of the past, colliding with the lurid reimagining in current favor.

The set, by Brian Thomson would give the appearance of a real cinema, the interior covered in dark blue canvas, scaffolding, and an apology for the inconvenience created during demolition projected on the movie screen. A string of bare bulbs would create the lightning, an old power box on the back wall at the side of the stage would become the "sonic transducer" as the "cinema," itself provided the props to tell the tale, in a form of swan song to the dying structure.

TD - What was the initial reaction to the show?

MJ - Nobody expected the nerve it struck with the audience. Expected to run for a month, it, instead, moved to a real cinema with a larger capacity, and when it was condemned, moved again to another cinema, where it would run for years.

TD - What happened next?

MJ - With so much Australian input, the next production was destined for Sydney, but when American music mogul, Lou Adler, showed interest in taking the show to Los Angeles to showcase his new nightclub, The Roxy, Sydney was delayed till the American show had been directed, with Sydney opening a couple of weeks after L.A.

TD - How did the Roxy engagement lead to your cousin, Paul Jabara, getting the role?

MJ - The L.A. venue was a small nightclub, seating 250, not a cinema, with a bar and table service. It resembled a cabaret more than the experience it had been in London, or was to be in Australia. The Roxy show ran for 9 months, with Tim Curry, London's original Frank 'N Furter, playing the first 6 months before leaving to return to England to make the motion picture version. He was replaced in the role at The Roxy, by Paul Jabara for the rest of the run.

TD - So The Roxy engagement got launched, but what happened in Australia? Did the show resume?

MJ - Yes, it was produced by Harry M. Miller. In Australia, the Frank N Furter role would be given to Reg Livermore, who had played Herod after the first year, in the Australian cast of "Jesus Christ Superstar". The title role of Rocky would be played by Graham Matters.

TD - How did the play do?

MJ - "The Rocky Horror Show" was a smash hit in Australia. Set in a rotting cinema in Globe, Sydney, it ran to packed houses for 18 months, before transferring to Melbourne for another 18 months, where a piece of the rainbow from Thomson's set for "Hair" was reused in the enormous incarnation of the "Rocky Horror" set in a venue that held over 700 at full capacity. At the time, Australia had a population of approximately 15 million, and so 3 years of sold-out performances was an amazing run for any show.

TD - How much of the production team and /or cast rolled over into the movie?

MJ - The motion picture was directed by Jim Sharman, designed by Brian Thomson, edited by Graeme Clifford, had Nell Campbell playing Columbia, and Rocky's voice was provided by Trevor White, all Australians. Sharman and Richard O'Brien co-wrote the screenplay based on O'Brien's stage play.

TD - Would there be competition for audiences for the show and the movie?

MJ - With the show packing houses in London and Sydney, the film was seen as lackluster and redundant. Harry M. Miller, with fear it may damage the show's ticket sales, had the film held back, until he had a private viewing and decided it would have no impact at all.

TD - Was the movie an instant success?

MJ - The only state where the film found instant success was my state, Queensland, where the show didn't play in any form until 1978. Opening at The Valley Twin, in Brisbane, mid-1976, the movie was outrageously popular, and played twice daily for 3 years, before transferring to a different cinema and becoming a once a week late night cult.

Queensland's embracing of the film was rewarded with a red vinyl LP release of the soundtrack in 1978, and the cinema was awarded a Platinum Record for their role in its popularity.

I saw the movie 26 times during the Valley Twin run, where there was no audience participation, apart from singing along and dancing in the aisles.

TD - How did you first learn of the live show in London?

MJ - I knew of the live show, as my mother had seen The Kings Road Show in London, when on a vacation, and I'd sat transfixed as she described the experience in detail. I bought the Australian Cast recording, and played it incessantly.

TD - And, then, you saw the live show for yourself?

MJ - When the show finally played in Brisbane, it wasn't of the caliber of the original Australian stagings, . I loved it, but it wouldn't be until 1982, that I got to see a version closer to the original, when a revival, starring London's final Frank, Daniel Abineri, and Perry Bedden in the role of Riff Raff, ran for a year.

This touring production was based on London's Comedy Theatre version, with a scaled-down set, without the canvas and scaffolding, and without Frank's signature entrance from the back of the theatre.

TD - Can you mention some highlights?

MJ - In 1984, a 10th anniversary production, with Reg Livermore, played Brisbane and Sydney. In Brisbane the show finally played in its full original form. In a dilapidated cinema, canvas-covered, scaffolding, and with a catwalk from the back of the room for Frank's entrance. It was what I'd waited for, a revelation, and my favourite incarnation. The show would retain the full set for the rest of its several tours, although the catwalk wouldn't be seen again, finishing in 1988.

The show was rewritten in 1990, and when the show returned to the Australian stage in 1992, it was no longer the same experience. It had become a celebration of the movie, and for me it lost the magic that had made me a fan.

The public, obviously, didn't feel the same, and this version would keep resurfacing for most of the 1990s.

TD - What type of "Rocky Horror" personal participation did you engage in?

MJ - When I realized the original show wasn't returning, I set about building a website to document and save information, stories, images, and videos of how it has been.

My website has been a labor of love and has introduced me to cast members, technical staff, and fans worldwide. Becoming friends with Perry Bedden, I was honored to work on his "Rocky Horror Picture Book", and travel to New York City with him to have dinner with Sal Piro. The 40th-anniversary convention in Manhattan gave me lifelong friends and the opportunity to spend time with

Patricia Quinn and Nell Campbell. When the show celebrated its 40th anniversary in Australia,

I was asked to contribute to the history written in the official program, and last year, I was interviewed for a German documentary.

TD - Do you have any final words?

MJ - It was great when it all began, and it still is."

Notes

1. interview with author 3/9/21

2. interview with author 3/6/21

Chapter 5
Two Midnight Movies
From Two Music Moguls

Learning how hard it is to make a movie succeed.

There's an apocryphal story in Hollywood that if you want your restaurant waiter's attention, you put your arm up and call "actor!". The point being that movie fever strikes many people, the way "Potomac Fever" infects aspiring politicos.

I worked with two music men that had ambitions of making it big in Hollywood and had lots in common with each other, but also vast differences.

One became a variation of the rags to riches Horatio Alger archetype, while the other was born with a silver spoon in his mouth that insulated him from financial hardship. The primary business of each was music and records, at which they excelled. Both had a failed movie that would become a legendary "midnight movie". Each used his music muscle as a lever into movie making. Both tried very hard to become movie, as well as music moguls. They had movie fever. In the end, they maintained their solid recognition as music moguls.

Lester Louis Adler and Christopher Percy Gordon Blackwell were born four years apart (1933 and 1937), in Chicago and London respectively, into very different circumstances and lifestyles. Both would eventually become legendary music producers, and aspiring movie makers. Each would have a very famous midnight movie (For Adler "The Rocky Horror Picture Show" -1975) and for Blackwell "The Harder They Come" - 1972) to their credit. Both were known for a musical style early in their career: "sunshine pop" (the sand

and surf music of Jan and Dean, and later the California dreaming sounds of The Mamas and The Papas) for Adler, and reggae (Bob Marley) for Blackwell, and both would, later in their careers, become identified with a singular, blockbuster musical talent. It was Carole King for Lou Adler, and U2 for Chris Blackwell.

Lou Adler was inducted into the Rock and Roll Hall of Fame in 2013, receiving the Ahmet Ertegun Award for Lifetime Achievement, while Blackwell received the same honor a dozen years earlier in 2001 (when it was called the Non-Performers Award, but renamed in honor of of Ahmet Ertegun in 2008).

That's where the similarities ended. Adler told me he was the son of a long-distance truck driver, while Blackwell was born to wealth and privilege as the son of Joseph Blackwell, one of the long line of Blackwells that provided sugar grown at the family's Jamaica sugarcane plantation to the centuries-old British establishment food company Crosse and Blackwell.

Having not only a wealthy father, his mother was an heiress to fortunes in Jamaican rum and sugarcane, and Costa Rican bananas. Chris showed me a childhood picture of himself seated on the verandah of his family's plantation house in Jamaica where he was surrounded by an army of black house servants. Lou's formative years, spent in the Boyle Heights neighborhood of East Los Angeles, could be considered hard and impoverished by any comparison.

Educated at the elite Harrow School (founded in 1572) Chris would have worn a formal morning suit to classes and be expected to have a top hat and cane as part of his schoolboy uniform. A who's who of British nobility and upper crust achievers would have been among his classmates.

Chris knew "society" but Lou knew "the streets", a decided advantage for him, and one of his greatest attributes that made working with him on "The Rocky Horror Picture Show" so interesting. The only other movie executive I dealt with that had Lou's organically intuitive touch for what was exactly right was Fox studio president Alan Ladd, Jr. Amazingly, they were both at Fox at the same time as me, one as a producer and the other as studio boss, but they never bonded, in fact never met: Lou came to the studio only once, for his initial meeting with the sales and marketing team. From then on, the studio went to Lou, who was not a socializer like many producers that kept offices at studios to be able to be part of that community. It was different for his music interests: he had an office at A+M Records, located in what had been Charlie Chaplin's movie studio.

Lou and Laddie missed the opportunity of making movies and history together which they surely would have, given the chance. That missed opportunity is a great "what if?" and could have turned Lou into the type of movie mogul he may have been aspiring to be, collaborating with a studio head that delivered seventeen Academy Award nominated or winner movies to Fox in the short span of just a few years.

Neither Lou nor Chris was a college graduate, although Adler, prophetically but briefly, attended Los Angeles City College to study journalism, where he met classmate Herb Alpert, who wanted to write songs. Lou told "Rolling Stone" in a 1968 interview, "At the time, I was dating Herb's wife, except they weren't married then, and it was through Sharon, I think, that Herb and I met. Herb asked me if I'd like to write some songs with him." (1) Their initial effort was writing "Wonderful World" ("Don't know much about history…") for Sam Cooke. Adler and Alpert went on to become lifelong colleagues and music legends. For a while, Alpert's A&M Records distributed records for Lou's Ode label.

My relationship with Chris Blackwell and his film interests was directly related to "The Rocky Horror Picture Show" and was a result of that movie. Like the reclusive Adler, who pretty much keeps to his Malibu estate's environs (except to famously sit next to Jack Nicholson at Lakers basketball games), Blackwell also kept out of sight, rarely visiting Los Angeles, so I was surprised when he called and asked to meet.

Chris wanted something from me and was urged by "The Rocky Horror Show" producer Michael White, Chris told me, to have me screen his new movie "Countryman" (1982) and see if I was interested in representing that film, and also his new movie division called Island Pictures that had an ambitious slate of movies lining up for production and release. Chris told me he received very little of the box-office profits from "The Harder They Come", a movie he had financially backed that became a famous midnight movie. He was determined to take a more active role with "Countryman" and have Island Pictures release the movie.

"Rocky Horror" executive producer (with Adler) Michael White, grateful for what I did for "The Rocky Horror Picture Show", had already linked me with another of his movies "Urgh: A Music War" (1981) which was a movie of a 1980 punk and new wave music concert filmed in Frejus, located in the Côte d'Azur, more popularly known as the French Riviera.

That movie, now a cult classic, blended both movie and music in the type of pop culture combination that Hollywood and Blackwell and Adler were aspiring to—success with musical products and success in the movies.

Coincidentally, I had already met with director Penelope Spheeris (thanks to an introduction by a mutual friend from my Fox Studio days) who was making "The Decline of Western

Civilization" (1981), her documentary about the Los Angeles punk rock scene. Spheeris would later reveal in her biography that "the LAPD Chief of Police Daryl Gates wrote a letter demanding the film 'not be shown again in the city' after a riotous Hollywood Boulevard theatrical screening. (2) It, too, went on to achieve cult status.

Being close to "The Rocky Horror Picture Show", "Urgh: A Music War", and "The Decline of Western Civilization", cult movies about punk and new wave music, and sci-fi transexuals began to make me feel like I was being transformed into someone that was automatically connected with cult pop culture, all because of my "Rocky Horror" success.

I knew I had to break out of that mold when the president of marketing at Metro-Goldwyn-Mayer invited me to the studio for a private screening of "Pink Floyd-The Wall" (1982) and in his office afterward asked me how MGM could create a "cult following" for the Pink Floyd movie. As nicely as I could, I suggested that Pink Floyd was already a super-cult band, that "The Wall" was one of their top albums, and that maybe MGM should just release it and let nature take its course, hoping the Pink Floyd fan base would show up without MGM trying to manipulate an audience for the movie.

You did not need to go to the movie to enjoy the music when you could do that by listening to the album at home, I added, so the logic of even turning the album into a movie was senseless except that it was what music people wanted: music and movie success, which circles back to the ambitions of Adler and Blackwell that, as good as they were at making record albums, they also wanted that sort of success as movie makers.

Going from a play to a movie and then a top-selling soundtrack was a creative and commercial trifecta that Lou Adler pulled off with "Rocky Horror", but few of his contemporaries have been able to have that sort of music and movie success.

Chris Blackwell got temporarily sidetracked out of movies when his Island Records group U2 suddenly emerged as the biggest group in music. He returned years later through Palm Pictures that generally served the DVD retailers, but he was not making movies for the theatrical market.

Lou made several movies, with "Up In Smoke" (1978) (which he directed) being a success and an example of how a recording act (comics Cheech and Chong) could translate to the screen, marking a victory for a brand extension by Lou of Cheech and Chong, if not unequivocally endorsing the concept that a music maker could become a movie maker.

It was the ambition of creating an ancillary market (moviegoers) and new revenue stream for an established musical product, by turning a musically-told narrative into a movie, that "Pink Floyd-The Wall" failed at. The opposite was true with "Rocky Horror".

As he industrialized "The Rocky Horror Picture Show" over the decades, Lou Adler became a master at creating "ancillaries" and "brand extensions" with a huge inventory of "Rocky Horror" branded products to sell, including music, books, a prequel that was billed as an "equal", and a remake of the original movie, several repackagings of the movie's soundtrack, as well as an endless line of impulse-buy "merch" that resembles what you see sold at arenas where music concerts are held. (see chapter "The Industrialization of 'Merch Madness'").

Adler and Blackwell both had important roles in fostering midnight movies, which had their natural origin in "The Harder They Come". Blackwell was there first, but Adler had the golden key: "The Rocky Horror Picture Show" was handled by a major studio with unchallenged strength as a theatrical distributor, and me as a persistent Fox executive that did everything possible to ensure success.

Blackwell did not have those resources and could not compete with a "major studio" in the business of booking theaters and collecting film rentals. This is what had hurt him with "The Harder They Come".

"The Harder They Come" was released in February 1973 through Roger Corman's New World Pictures as "blaxploitation", a new genre that featured mostly African-American actors in urban-set action movies. (3)

The groundbreaking "Shaft" (1971) gave Hollywood hope that it was onto something with this subgenre of action-adventure movies, but this genre eventually fizzled.

Loaded with hypnotic reggae music, and a laid back vibe, "The Harder They Come" was miscast as action-adventure blaxploitation, and dropped by New World Pictures. The fact that it was also criticized as "the first English language movie in history to require subtitles in the United States" (4), thanks to its heavy Jamaican patois, hurt it's chances of connecting with an audience, until it was adopted by stoned college kids and eventually migrated to midnight screenings.

Like "The Rocky Horror Picture Show", "The Harder They Come" was a box office failure until reborn as a midnight movie. It helped to promote reggae in the United States that Bob Marley was becoming known as a reggae superstar, thanks to Chris Blackwell whose Island Records released Marley's "Catch a Fire" album in April 1973, almost simultaneously to the release of the movie.

Although Marley had made prior records, this was the first album to be handled by Blackwell, who became an advocate of reggae music through Marley, whose songs would drive the narrative in "Countryman". But, even that did not help make a musical project (Marley) into a movie hit ("Countryman").

Eventually, the movie's director/writer Perry Henzell took over distribution himself, and turned "The Harder They Come" into a midnight success that gained a campus reputation. In Cambridge, Massachusetts, the movie ran for six years at midnight, at the Orson Welles Cinema, a record that lasted several years until "The Rocky Horror Picture Show" swept into the midnight market and has retained dominance there for over four decades of continuous play.

Lou Adler and I never spoke about "The Harder They Come" or about his parallel path with Chris Blackwell, and I never spoke to Chris about Lou and "Rocky Horror" except to verify Michael White's recommendation of me. However, it was a unique experience for me to have worked with two men that had such similar paths from music to movies, trying to break out of one silo (music) and into another silo (movies), just as Hollywood was trying to blend music and movies into a shared entertainment opportunity, but never really achieved the hoped-for cross-over.

Lou tried his hand at both music and movies through 14 projects over a 23 year period (1958-1981). Of that creative inventory, five were movies that made it to the big screen, not straight to cable, or to video on demand, or "streamers" like many of today's movies. They were "Monterey Pop" (1967), "Brewster McCloud" (1970), "The Rocky Horror Picture Show" (1975), "Up In Smoke" (1978), and "Shock Treatment" (1981). That adds an authenticity to his role as a movie maker.

After a thirty-five year absence, in which he was involved in what he has called "my greatest productions" (5) his seven sons, Lou returned to filmed entertainment when he and Kenny Ortega tried to reimagine "The Rocky Horror Picture Show" with the made-for-tv

"The Rocky Horror Picture Show: Let's Do the Time Warp Again" that was broadcast in 2016.

An exception to the challenge both Adler and Blackwell faced in trying to become hyphenated moguls (music and movies) is David Geffen, a bona fide cross-over music and movies mogul, and a spectacular one at that.

Geffen founded the record labels Asylum Records, and Geffen Records, and in movies he co-founded DreamWorks Pictures with Steven Spielberg and Jeffrey Katzenberg. Lou Adler is the only music legend that comes close to playing in the Geffen music and movie mogul ballpark.

To be big in both music and movies is not impossible, it's just hard.

Notes:

1. https://www.rollingstone.com/music/music-news/lou-adler-california-dreamin-75011/.

2. http://penelopespheeris.com/bio.html

3. https://www.bfi.org.uk/news-opinion/news-bfi/lists/10-great-blaxploitation-movies

4. [Bordowitz, Hank, Every Little Thing Gonna Be Alright: The Bob Marley Reader, Da Capo, 2009, p. 58. — https://en.wikipedia.org/wiki/The_Harder_They_Come

5. https://jewishjournal.com/uncategorized/214558/lou-adler-low-key-lucky-and-very-cool/)

Chapter 6
Fox Acquires
"The Rocky Horror Picture Show"

The secret deal that made it happen.

Being like the struggle of Sisyphus, who pushed a rock up a hill only to have it roll back down on him over and over, might describe the challenges that "The Rocky Horror Picture Show" producers Lou Adler and Michael White faced with 20th Century-Fox Film Corporation as the studio that would handle their movie.

Once the studio acquired distribution rights, only after very quietly compromising those rights, the struggle continued through a poorly-received screening at the studio for the executives, an uncertain initial executive planning meeting for how to release the movie theatrically, a disastrous sneak preview in Santa Barbara, and then a first run theatrical release in Los Angeles that lost money and led to the shelving of the movie and pulling the soundtrack out of stores.

I was at all four events: the screening, meeting, and sneak. I was also part of this core group that saw the stage play at The Roxy as an initial introduction to "Rocky Horror"; a preview that made a poor impression on the studio team.

Redemption came only with the midnight show that would bring the movie and its music back from the dead, and become the key that unlocked the flood of profits, and the creation of a pop culture event. The movie and its soundtrack went on to have phenomenal commercial performance in one of the most long-lived and successful synergies of movie and music in Hollywood history, an accomplishment never matched before or since.

36

But that all came later. It began with a call to Lou Adler in Bel Air from his girlfriend and mother of their infant child Nikolai, Britt Ekland, who lived in London. Richard O'Brien, a New Zealander who had written a musical called "The Rocky Horror Show" that Michael White premiered on June 19, 1973 at the Royal Court Theater (Upstairs) in London before moving to a bigger venue. It was a success.

The Swedish movie star and "Bond girl" Ekland was one of its many fans. She encouraged Lou to see it when he came to London to see their son.

As Britt recalled it, she "first saw 'The Rocky Horror Show' at the Classic Cinema on Kings Road [in]… early fall 1973". At the time, she knew her boyfriend was "looking for something special to put into The Roxy Theatre in LA" where Lou was part owner. She followed her instinct that this show would be perfect with its "ingenious" music, and "perfect" performances. She recalls that, "it is very seldom [one] get[s] the feeling of having been part of something so totally new and revolutionary" as 'Rocky Horror' has proved to be."

When Lou came to London they "attended a party given by American film producer Hercules Belleville [and] Lou was introduced to 'The Rocky Horror Show' producer Michael White…[they] started the conversations that would lead to an agreement that would bring 'The Rocky Horror Show' to the Roxy". And as time has shown, Lou "came, he saw and the rest is history!" (1)

Six months after The Roxy opened, "The Rocky Horror Show" opened on March 21, 1974, and ran for several months before the cast left for England to film the movie, pending getting a studio deal to take it as a "negative pick-up".

37

A "negative pick-up" was a popular format in the seventies where a studio would acquire the distribution rights for a movie that was to be independently produced. For a pre-negotiated price, the filmmaker would deliver to the studio a finished negative of the movie and the studio would make release prints, book theaters, and set and pay for a marketing plan.

Production costs were covered by the acquisition purchase price. The risk of distribution was on the studio, so they ultimately could pull the plug whenever they saw failure. A negative pick-up protected the studio's downside (potential loss) and rewarded it with a share of the upside (profits).

A studio's acquisition payment would fund the production of the movie, and the studio would book it into theaters and pay for the prints and ads. Those distribution costs, and the pre-paid acquisition cost, and a distribution fee would be recouped by the studio before the producers received profits.

In terms of studio pride in the movie, a negative pickup barely reached the threshold of orphan because the studio had no skin in the game. It was not a Fox production, developed by Fox, or made with Fox money. The producers were effectively "renting" Fox to release the movie through their sales department, and using Fox money to support media buys. For this, the studio would recoup their advertising costs and "acquisition" price and take a distribution fee.

In risk-adverse Hollywood it became a formula where bets could be hedged and studios could concentrate on their homegrown ideas, using negative pick-ups to round out the annual release schedule.

In his search for a taker for his negative pick-up deal, Lou Adler approached Fox. "I spoke to (Gordon) Stulberg...a former partner at the law firm that I was repped by...he brought his wife, to the show...we papered it....that did it..." as if the deal had been simply consummated and memorialized on a cocktail napkin from the Roxy nightclub. (2)

It got a little more complicated. Lou did invite the Fox president to The Roxy to see the show. Stulberg came with more than his wife, Helen Stulberg. At his direction, several of us executives from the production, sales and marketing teams were also in the audience that night. None of us who gathered in the Roxy driveway after the show, including me, had walked out of The Roxy saying "we've got to take this deal and release this movie".

Adler, an independent producer not privy to internal studio deliberations of what to do about his potential movie, walked away from the evening saying "I don't think he (Stulberg) understood the motivation for the reaction, but from what he saw he was enthused enough to spend one-million-dollars" to acquire distribution rights. (3)

The final budget would be $1.3 million.

Scott Stulberg remembers "What my mom told me at the time, when I was a teenager, is that Lou Adler told my dad 'come see this play-you gotta come see this-you're going to want to make it into a movie'. Lou gave him front row seats at The Roxy for my mom and dad. Mom told me that after the play ended, my dad looked at her and asked "what did you think", to which mom said "absolutely yes!". (4)

That pillow talk went only so far. It stayed in the bedroom suite, never making it to the studio executive suites. Inside the studio walls the reaction was negative. Stulberg polled his executives. "Laddie (production VP Alan Ladd, Jr.) didn't want to touch it" recalled production executive Bob Sherman, neither did production head Jere Henshaw. (5)

Sales head Peter Myers and marketing head Jonas Rosenfield, the men I worked with daily, wanted nothing to do with booking or selling this movie about "Sweet Transvestites from Transexual Transylvania".

With this negative feedback from at least two of his production executives and the sales and marketing leaders, Stulberg sent Sherman to see the play.

"Gordon Stulberg called me from a business trip he was on in Asia and asked me to go to The Roxy and see the show. I called him after seeing it and told him Fox should take it." (6)

Stulberg said keep moving the project forward.

It was left to Sherman to lead the conversation with Adler and Michael White. That led to an exploratory meeting at Sherman's Brentwood home on a Sunday afternoon where Sherman says Adler "pitched" the movie to him. Also there were Fox business affairs head Bill Immerman, and what he called "a couple of Brits" including impresario Michael White who had staged the play in London.

The deal points, recounted by Sherman, were that the "producers would have exclusive control over casting, and production". Sherman told Stulberg that those were non-negotiable points from the producers. The acquisition cost was to be $1.3 million.

Sherman "told Gordon Stulberg to take the movie", trying to push him off the fence and easing his hesitations. As thanks, Sherman says that Adler "gifted me with a statue of one of the girls that gets zapped at the end of the movie." (7) Adler remembers, saying "I gave Bob Sherman a cast of one of the girls from the end of the movie" (8)

I had always known that Bob Sherman was central to the acquisition process. Very serendipitously at a Beverly Hills lunch with a small group that included former head of the Warner Brothers studio Bob Shapiro, a good friend of Sherman, I was able to access Sherman through Shapiro, who made the introduction for me.

Sherman's important role in getting the movie to Fox, clarified in my interview with him, answered one of the key questions I had about the movie's acquisition by Fox. I knew there was a production executive who advocated to Stulberg to acquire the movie and then led the Fox team that made the deal that Stulberg ultimately signed off on.

I viewed it as an important missing link, but couldn't draw out from Adler who that was. It was Bob Sherman.

While Sherman and I were at Fox simultaneously, and each had offices in the executive building, we never crossed paths. By the time I got involved with the movie, after it was filmed, Sherman had left to produce "The Missouri Breaks" (1976).

Until Sherman and I spoke, Adler had been steadfast in his narrative that it was an easy sell to Fox and that it was just him and Stulberg that made it happen. Sherman, while important and supportive at a critical moment, has existed only in the shadows for five decades.

Once I found Sherman, and learned of his role in acquiring the movie, the scholarship expanded by learning from Sherman how concerned Stulberg was about making the acquisition, and what turned out to be a financially hurtful deal for Fox in order to get the movie, once Stullberg gave it a green light.

In the end, Stulberg stayed on the fence. He was willing to take the movie but only after he very quietly lined up an outside financier put up cash to lessen the financial exposure and risk for Fox. That man, John Heyman, would later say that "The Rocky Horror Picture Show" was one of the most successful movie investments he ever made. (9)

When I shared this with Adler fifty years after the movie went into production, that the studio had so little faith in the movie that it was willing to sell off some of its equity interest and potential profits to hedge their bet, Lou expressed surprise, telling me that "I don't recall meeting or being aware of other money sources at that time." (10)

Had the studio president revealed to the marketing and sales team, a group that already wanted nothing to do with the movie, that he recruited an outside investor to help offset the distribution risk, it may have caused those executives to use it as a reason for not giving the movie even minimal attention.

If producers Adler and White were informed that Fox had so little faith in the idea of the movie that it was selling off some of the ownership rights, the producers could have easily seen this as a message of non-confidence and could have taken their movie to another studio.

Both Stulberg and Sherman left Fox before the finished movie was delivered. There was nobody left in the production department that had been involved in the acquisition negotiations who would have known about the John Hayman investment. For me, and for historical accuracy, the mystery of Sherman's role has been solved.

Notes:

1. to author 2/22/19

2. to author 11/19/2018

3. Page 19 "The Rocky Horror Picture Show Book, Bill Henkin, Hawthorn Books, NY 1979

4. interview with author 3/9/2020

5. interview with author 1/12/23

6. ibid

7. ibid

8. to author 1/12/23

9. interview with author 1/12/23

10. to author 11/13/2023

Chapter 7
Introducing "The Rocky Horror Picture Show" to Moviegoers

The Fateful Theatrical Release

What to do with or how to handle "The Rocky Horror Picture Show?" was a question that stumped and scared the marketing and sales teams at the 20th Century Fox Film Corporation, even during production. They were totally unprepared to venture into explaining to theater owners and movie audiences why they should book a ticket, or attend a movie about "Sweet transvestites from Transexual Transylvania."

Was Fox the right place for "The Rocky Horror Picture Show?" Was any big Hollywood studio the right place for the picture? Today, every studio has a "Speciality," which means a division to market less than mainstream movies. In the mid-70's, the marketing and distribution were homogeneous: every movie was handled by the same teams in the same proven ways. How to release a studio movie in the early 1970's wasn't much different from how they did it in the 1940's Golden Age.

Ideally, this was a movie that was perfectly suited for handling by the legendary Don Rugoff and his Cinema V Company. Rugoff was, "One of the seminal figures in the 1960s art cinema world…he initiated key aspects of marketing, distribution, and strategy that would influence other regimes of independent cinema through the decades". (1)

Don Rugoff was a vertically integrated entrepreneur as an art film distributor and exhibitor with control of most of the leading art houses in Manhattan (The Cinema I, II and III, Paris, Plaza, Sutton,

Beekman, Paramount, Murray Hill, Gramercy, and Art theaters) that served as an infrastructure for his brilliant creativity in handling hard to handle movies. Borrowing from Frank Sinatra, according to him Rugoff, was a helluva man, "If you can make it there, you can make it anywhere."

Some of the better-known of the dozens of Rugoff released films include, "The Endless Summer", "Elvira Madigan", "Z,", "The Sorrow and the Pity", "Putney Swope", "The Firemen's Ball", "Trash," "The Garden of the Finzi-Continis", "Gimme Shelter", "The Hellstrom Chronicle", "On Any Sunday", "Greaser's Palace","Cesar and Rosalie","The Tall Blond Man with One Black Shoe", "Scenes From a Marriage", "Going Places", "Swept Away", "Monty Python and the Holy Grail", "Seven Beauties", and "The Man Who Fell to Earth". (2)

Rugoff had such a solid lock on the speciality-art-indie film world that no studio could even come close to his capabilities of how to manage specialized, offbeat, or challenging films like "The Rocky Horror Picture Show".

Conversely, studios did not get these types of films because Rugoff's reputation drew indie and art filmmakers used to approach him before they approached the studios.

Today, all studios have segmented distribution divisions; some teams work on major release tentpole movies and franchise releases, while other teams work on movies harvested at film festivals. And the midnight release slot became a routine booking once studios saw how successful after "Rocky Horror",

Did Lou Adler's distribution deal with Fox for "Rocky Horror" come too easily? Did he know what he was getting into at the studio? Could it be a caveat emptor cautionary tale? His Fox deal came with no auction or shopping around, or investigation, that may have uncovered Cinema V and Don Rugoff.

An assessment of Fox at the time showed very few bright spots. The most noteworthy studio accomplishment was not success at the box office but at the negotiating table resulting in a settlement of a hostile takeover bid by Broadway producer David Merrick, who was the largest individual shareholder of Fox. He was asking for five seats on the board and rumbled about either a proxy fight or a tender offer to purchase the studio (3)

When producer Frank McCarthy pitched Fox studio head Daryl F. Zanuck to make "Patton" (1970), on October 21, 1951 cable reply from the mogul was, "Get going on it".In his acceptance speech when he won the Academy Award for Best Picture, McCarthy said, "It took nineteen years to make this movie". (4)

Lou was not in the mold of McCarthy, who was a producer, like many, who invested years of effort to get a movie made. It was only two years (1973-75) between Fox saying "yes" to Adler and the start of production to opening day at the UA Westwood.

Time beats faster in the music world. Did this create an impatience in Lou to spend time finding exactly the right distributor, one where his friends who knew the movie industry may have given him some insights or an introduction to the hottest studio heads at the time, John Calley at Warner Brothers and Robert Evans at Paramount? Was Lou on such a fast track that he went with the first yes he got instead of using that to leverage a better deal elsewhere?

In the record business, which would have been Lou's frame of reference, a germ of an idea for a single can be developed and produced as a record and released to radio and retail in days, and a full album in mere months. This is why records have traditionally been more relevant to pop culture than movies. The arc from a thought to a finished product takes exponentially longer when it's a movie, and by the time that movie is released the original premise may have become outdated.

"Music moves the needle culturally more than movies do," said film critic Elvis Mitchell, who added that "music has cultural momentum and is the center of gravity in this culture." (5)

While this may differentiate movies from music, the production and distribution processes are similar. You need a personal attachment and investment from the top to push your project through the system. You rarely get that from a "suit," and Lou's Fox deal was with an executive who was a lawyer, not a creative production executive like Calley or Evans.

Adler's deal to release "Rocky Horror" through Fox was made with a simplicity as if it were a note on a cocktail napkin. "I spoke to (Gordon) Stulberg.. a former partner at the law firm that I was repped by...he brought his wife to the show...we papered it....that did it..." is the over-simplified history provided by Adler (6)

Fox would soon get its own Calley/Evans in Alan Ladd, Jr., popularly known throughout Hollywood as Laddie, but he only became studio head after "Rocky Horror" failed at the box office and was shelved.

Lou invited a group of Fox studio executives, including me, to the live stage play of "Rocky Horror," at The Roxy, his Sunset Strip nightclub. Most of us from Fox, including me, didn't like what we saw.

The sale may have been influenced by Helen Stulberg, wife of the studio head, who liked it and encouraged her husband to buy the rights to distribute the movie. As her son Scott recalled, "What my mom told me at the time when I was a teenager, is that Lou Adler told my dad 'come see this play—you gotta come see this—you're going to want to make it into a movie'. Lou gave him front-row seats at The Roxy for my mom and dad." He continued, "Mom told me that after the play ended, my dad looked at her and asked, 'What did you think?' to which mom said, 'Absolutely yes!'" (7) The mis-fit at Fox started to become apparent once the deal was made.

The good news for Lou Adler about the Fox deal quickly dissipated when Gordon Stulberg suddenly left the studio during production, and a "Troika" of three top executives took over Fox. Laddie (Alan Ladd, Jr.) was one of the three executive vice presidents now running the studio, and would quickly become studio president and the man who greenlighted "Star Wars" (1975), and would give me the green light to release "Rocky Horror" at midnight.

The departure of Stulberg left Lou without a personal contact at the studio that was now obligated to release his movie. How to succeed in Hollywood could be summed up in one word, and that's not script, star, or director. It's "relationships," and now, with Stulberg gone, Lou was friendless at Fox.

The movie was a "negative pickup" in which the studio had no direct investment in production, even though it had not been involved in scripting or casting, and had no production vice president assigned to it to shepherd it through the studio. All these factors helped contribute to the "Orphan" status of "The Rocky Horror Picture Show," at Fox.

Despite the executive suite turmoil, the movie continued with filming, and Lou invited Fox's European sales and marketing executives to watch the filming, near London, of the climactic swimming pool scene. "There was dead silence," he said. "They didn't stay for lunch." (8)

The Fox executives had never seen anything quite like this movie, and their reluctance to bond with it, that was revealed very early during production, would continue through the distribution process that included a screening at the studio for the executives, a sneak preview in Santa Barbara, and a first run theatrical release in Los Angeles.

When Lou eventually screened the movie for Fox executives at the studio, a screening I attended, the reaction was cold: "When it ended...nobody said a word...then they quickly walked out...." (9)

Following the screening, Lou came to a meeting at Fox to hear from the sales and marketing teams what they planned to do with his movie. As he went around the room, he did not hear much from anybody until he got to me. I was much younger than my colleagues and related to him in a way that the suited executives did not.

He was casual by comparison, with his long hair and beard, shorts, Hawaiian shirt, and espadrilles, the signature hippie look that I saw a lot of in rustic, free-spirited Topanga Canyon, where I lived next to an ashram.

I told him I didn't like the movie; he said I could therefore be objective; that's how and when I became the studio's point person to deal with Lou Adler and "The Rocky Horror Picture Show."

The negative trend continued when Fox brought the movie to Santa Barbara, a coastal community ninety miles north of LA, for what turned into a disastrous sneak preview. "A good two-thirds of the audience walked out on it," remembered Adler. "Afterwards, we were sitting on the curb, as dejected as any filmmaker who had been with the project for so long." (10)

By then, it appeared that I was the only Fox executive who professionally believed in the movie's possibilities, even though I personally did not like it.

49

"Tim Deegan was with the project from the beginning," said Adler. "He sat on the curb with me outside the theater in Santa Barbara. The only glimmer of hope was that there were four or five people who sat through it and came up after the film and thanked us for making that kind of film. We were really happy. It was almost like we made it for someone." (11)

Where and how to open "The Rocky Horror Picture Show," was a critical decision, as it is with every movie. The first booking of a movie can set the tone for its theatrical release, telegraphing to the audience, the critics, and other theater operators the studio's position and belief in a movie.

Some movies call for national saturation in thousands of theaters at once supported by a massive media buy, some roll out slowly in order to build an audience, and others open very small in just a few theaters to reach a more specialized indie or art house audience.

"Rocky Horror" fit into the indie-art house category, but that's not how Fox approached the theatrical release. Initially, until what was a bad plan was cancelled, the release strategy was exploitation.

The negative sneak previewed in Santa Barbara and a studio sales and marketing team that had clearly admitted they had no idea what to do with the movie and no interest in it, hinted at trouble for the release.

I was included in the planning conversations about where and how to open the movie because I had become the sole studio executive contact with Adler. The most obvious choice was Los Angeles, where success in the number two movie market could be a strong endorsement of the movie, but that came with a significant downside.

The stage play ("The Rocky Horror Show") had run for nine months at The Roxy, Adler's new club on the Sunset Strip, where it became a huge hit. While this would give us a built-in awareness of the title in LA, if it did well at the box office, exhibitors around the country could easily say it was because of the Roxy experience.

Fox needed to book a market that would be more credible than Los Angeles. New York, the number one movie market in the country, was an obvious choice, but Adler demurred because the stage play had been a failure on Broadway.

That didn't stop the studio from making a plan, created by the studio's publicity department headed by Johnny Friedkin, that pitched ad-pub VP Jonas Rosenfield and sales VP Peter Myers to open the movie in the New York market in Long Island City, which is located in the borough of Queens, across the East River from the borough of Manhattan.

They suggested a publicity campaign built around the slogan "Now All Queens Can See The Rocky Horror Picture Show." I thought this was a very tacky approach, and would limit our audience that I hoped would be college kids going to see this as a goofy, date-night entertainment.

I went to the only man in the sales department I had any regular contact with, which was Ashley Boone who, a few years later, would mastermind the release of "Star Wars" for Laddie. For now, he was the western regional sales manager that had oversight of all theater bookings from the Rockies west to the Pacific, and I, as the Los Angeles advertising manager, had oversight of all advertising in LA, the studio's second-largest market, so we met together often and had an easy relationship.

Lou had not yet been looped into the "queens" strategy because I was afraid he might lose total confidence in how Fox proposed to handle his movie, and he had already asked that we stay away from New York altogether. Little did anyone know that "Rocky Horror" would conquer New York the minute the midnight show opened at the Waverly the following year.

An advantage of opening in LA was it would give Lou the opportunity to be 100% involved in every move we made, which I prioritized. To not take advantage of his input would be cutting out a very valuable asset. And, because I supervised the studio's advertising in LA, nothing would happen that I didn't know about and had a voice in.

Boone, like me, was distrustful of the movie being put into the hands of decision-makers who had no idea what to do with it, and together, we worked out a Los Angeles release plan to open at the UA Westwood in the bustling neighborhood for UCLA and its thousands of students.

I used this shift in booking plans to plead that the Fox publicity department (that had come up with the "queens" campaign) be taken off the movie. I miraculously got the authority to engage a local boutique publicity agency and was given a budget to pay for them and their plans.

Pulling off the exclusion of the studio's publicity department from a lead position in promoting "Rocky Horror" gave me confidence that my bosses were serious about giving me some responsibility for "Rocky Horror," and expanded my contact with Adler as I built that relationship.

While the LA planning had eyes-on and participation by Adler, it was an opportunity for me to put the movie under my thumb; it marked the start of my operational control of how Fox handled the movie from then on.

Now that the first booking was set, a marketing campaign had to be created, mainly a trailer and a poster. The chapter "Those Lips-

Building a Brand (Five Stories Behind the Iconic 'Rocky Horror' Lips)" fully explores this. We also needed a publicity program.

With the Fox publicity department taken off the picture and with a publicity budget I could control, I hired a small Los Angeles publicity firm called Proper Exposure (headed by Marykay Powell and Susan Pile), and they got right to work with the underground campaign, guerrilla marketing and wild posting using Peter Zachery's Creative Distributors team, not the traditional routine of making a big media splash for Los Angeles openings.

As Powell and Pile recounted, "We felt confident that we could handle [find the audience for] this extraordinary 'little' film, and they were right. The UA Westwood opening, with their role on the team, was very successful. (12)

They proved to be the equal of anything the benched Fox publicity department could have offered. The thinking and execution by Pile and Powell (an Andy Warhol protege and studio publicist, respectively) were attuned to the "underground" and "counterculture" instead of the mass audiences studios relied on to generate big box-office results.

In the mid-70s, in Los Angeles, it was possible to blend together an effective marketing campaign using wild posting, FM radio spots and promotions, and ads in alternative newspapers. Marykay and Susan knew how to reach the mid-70s version of what we today call "social media influencers."

Lou Adler released the soundtrack to coincide with the opening at the UA Westwood, which promoted the movie from a complementary angle.

Without these elements of guerrilla marketing and a soundtrack release, I'm not sure we would have had the strong Los Angeles opening that we did. The feel they gave to the campaign was more like what was happening in the music business... street-level marketing that was targeting an "underground" audience.

A sense of exclusivity to the UA Westwood opening was the corollary to the "underground" marketing campaign. Pre-selling tickets to opening night was the hook that blended two sales techniques, one from the music world and another old-school format of how showcased movies used to be sold.

Concerts and clubs routinely sold advance tickets to their attractions. "Why couldn't this be done for the Los Angeles opening of the movie?", asked regional sales executive Ashley Boone.

Adler and I supported it, but it was something studios had stopped doing decades earlier when movies were presented as "roadshows," which were advance-sale reserved show engagements that helped give a movie special attraction status. Ashley was able to convince UA theaters that the advance sales would be successful enough to offset a reduction in advertising to attract an opening night audience. It was a quirky way to go, but that added to the allure.

Another part of the plan was to screen the movie for highly targeted press but he asked them to embargo their reviews until after opening night. Studios and press had a gentleman's agreement for this type of treatment. It was generally understood that a studio asking for a pre-release embargo was nervous about what the critics may say.

Studios and media critics had a positive, symbiotic relationship. Each needed the other (the papers wanted the movie advertising buys, and the studios wanted the publicity from writers covering the movies), so compromising was not unusual. Even with that, it did not mean a free pass on a review.

The carefully selected press were invited to the one and only press screening, which was held in the Little Theater on the Fox lot.

When "Rocky Horror" did open in regular release at the UA in Westwood on Sept. 26, 1975, "It did fairly well because it had a reputation and somewhat of a following," said Adler. "I don't recall reading many reviews, but there weren't many raves, I can tell you that." (13)

When the movie was playing Lou and I, or sometimes just one or the other of us, would sit in the audience at the UA Westwood to gauge audience reaction. We both noticed something unusual that we both mentioned in our interviews for Bill Henkin's book, which was published a few years after the first-midnight show and has become a definitive early text of the "Rocky Horror" phenomenon. I told Henkin that, "I could see a real hardcore audience developing," (14)

For Adler, it was trying to filter out negative reports from the theater: "You could go blind listening to the exhibitor. They'd say 'nothing's happening,' the theater holds 800 seats, and we're only getting fifty people,' but what they didn't tell you was the same fifty people coming back". (15)

Although Ashley Boone would begin to be absorbed with the planning for releasing "Star Wars' (1977), he kept an eye on the UA Westwood booking and also helped get a college market booking in Columbus (Ohio State University), but that became another failure. He was the only person in the sales department that had any interest in the movie. But that lasted only as long as the box office showed signs of life.

Lou Adler's sensitivity about how his movie should be positioned, the proven success of the boutique publicity agency Proper Exposure headed by Marykay Powell and Susan Pile, the advance ticket sale components of the awareness campaign, and a soundtrack record being merchandised and promoted by the record label provided a template that could have rolled out into additional markets.

Unfortunately, for a continued theatrical run of the movie, Ashley faced corporate pressure to pull the movie from release when it became apparent the one point three million dollar acquisition cost was offset by just a half-million dollars at the box office, which the studio got only a cut of so, by the all-important "film rental" measurement, the movie was a financial failure even though there was a small, devoted audience for the movie.

It was Boone, by then the assistant general sales manager, who gave me the heads up that he was recommending that the movie be pulled from release due to lagging box-office and a failed college test market. His decision, and the Fox chairman's demand that the Fox name be taken off the marketing that he characterized as "lewd and lascivious," meant the end of a theatrical release for "The Rocky Horror Picture Show."

I was sorry to lose Boone as a "Rocky Horror" ally, especially months later when I had to fight so hard to get the studio to reconsider the movie's shelving and try it as a midnight show.

By then, Ashley was unapproachable on practically anything except the all-consuming lead-up to "Star Wars," and his sales department colleagues would not take my calls or requests for a meeting about "Rocky Horror."

The economic engine based on Richard O'Brien's underlying intellectual property, called, "The Rocky Horror Show," ground to a halt. While the stage play would continue, there would be no more movie or music revenue. Along with a shutdown movie, Lou and Columbia Records pulled the soundtrack from release.

The tens-of-millions of dollars in profits from the movie and the record would only come later with the midnight show.

I was suddenly alone at Fox but persistent about what I wanted to do, which was the midnight release.

A few years earlier, when I was a teenager, I had been an intern for Stanley Kubrick when he released "2001: A Space Odyssey" at MGM. That experience gave me an insider, front-row seat to see how that movie, which had initially been a box office failure, was brought back from the dead by Mike Kaplan, a persistent young studio executive who would not give up on the movie. He got critics to re-review it. That inspired me to do something like that myself one day. I saw bringing "The Rocky Horror Picture Show," back from the dead as my opportunity.

I returned on a Saturday afternoon to my Topanga Canyon home after hiking high in the Santa Monica Mountains with my friends and got a phone call from Laddie, who I knew only by sight. He had recently become president of the studio and said he had heard that I was having trouble with my bosses about wanting to go midnight with "Rocky Horror." I had become very vocal to anyone who would listen, and even when they would not, so no doubt he had caught wind of my temper, which I used to buttress my cause. I got so loud and argumentative in one boardroom meeting about wanting to go at midnight that the CEO came in from his adjoining office to find out what was happening.

Laddie obliquely indicated there were going to be some big changes now that he was in charge and specifically stated, "I want you to be on my team, " which assured me that there was hope for my plans. Laddie's closing words were something like, "If you need any help with what you want to do, just come and see me." I eventually did, and in just a few minutes, he gave me the green light to take "The Rocky Horror Picture Show," to midnight.

When that happened, several months after the movie was shelved, Laddie's only question was my box office forecast from the midnight shows. Fox had never released a movie at midnight (no studio ever had before this), so there were no comparisons available. I confidently projected $5 million. "Go ahead and try it," he said. (16)

Not long after, there was a management shakeup by Laddie that saw most of my old bosses leave the studio, and I was pretty much left on my own to go forward with opening "The Rocky Horror Picture Show" at midnight. By now, everyone knew that when I talked about "Rocky Horror," I meant business and had the backing from Laddie.

Notes:

1. https://www.washingtonpost.com/archive/lifestyle/1990/10/2 6/the-horror-of-it-all/f9c47219-3af2-4628-b955-447624d2ca63/)

2. https://www.latimes.com/archives/la-xpm-1990-10-14-ca-3748-story.html)

3. Powell Interview with author 1/20/21

4. https://www.latimes.com/archives/la-xpm-1990-10-14-ca-3748-story.html)

5. source: Page 25 "The Rocky Horror Picture Show Book, Bill Henkin, Hawthorn Books, NY 1979).

6. ibid

7. source: Documentary film "Laddie: The Man Behind the Movies" 2019. https://www.imdb.com/title/tt4214198/).

Chapter 8
Back from the Dead
The Rocky Road to Midnight

The epic struggle to turn a failed movie into a midnight show.

Time Magazine has called the trade paper Variety "The Bible of show business" which has always been its reputation. (1) In his 2015 article about the 40th anniversary of "The Rocky Horror Picture Show," Variety's Tim Gray provided some scope to the financial footprint of the midnight show, as of that moment, when he reported that "Rocky Horror" was "earning more than $100 million in the U.S". (2) Gray's reporting was just for the midnight show up to 2015, and it does not include at least twenty versions of the soundtrack album and CD, home video and DVD sales, or any of the vast, related merchandise. That was several years ago; the enterprise continues unabated, and the profits continue to grow as the movie marks its fiftieth anniversary of continuous play.

What began as a $1,300,000 production budget has become an explosion of movie and soundtrack profits, all detonated by the midnight show. What follows is how that failed and shelved movie became such a success. It could be a Harvard Business School case study on how to grow and sustain an entertainment business enterprise, starting with giving a failed consumer product a new branding and a second chance in the marketplace.

A man who knows something about successful movies, Francis Ford Coppola, has said that, "When a movie is first made and is about to be released, you know that whatever the reaction is will define it for its entire life". (3)

By that standard, "The Rocky Horror Picture Show" deserved to die the death of a failed movie, for it barely found an audience when it opened at the UA Westwood theater in Los Angeles. And when it did sell tickets, it could have been to the people who had seen the play or being a repeat viewer.

The movie was a paradox. It failed in a first-run theatrical engagement but became a sold-out midnight show in New York and other cities across the country for five decades. It has become one of the greatest box office turnarounds ever in movie history, comparable to the way Stanley Kubrick's "2001: A Space Odyssey" (1968) found an audience after being an initial box-office bust. Originally a failure, "The Rocky Horror Picture Show" has been transformed into the longest continuously running theatrical movie ever. It's a theatrical record that will never be broken.

But, before that could happen, the movie had to be certified as dead, which Fox was only too happy to do.

The day suddenly came when Fox took "The Rocky Horror Picture Show" out of release. There was a lack of support by a studio management that had never truly backed the movie which was considered an orphan without a studio executive to advocate for it. Its only champions had been the studio president Gordon Stulberg who signed the acquisition deal with producers Lou Adler and Michael White, and production executive Robert Sherman. Both men had left Fox by the time Adler delivered the finished movie for release.

The electrocardiogram-like graph of the ups and downs of "Rocky Horror" would eventually define the "Rocky Horror" trident that includes the stage play, the movie, and the soundtrack record.

Richard O'Brien's 1973 stage play ("The Rocky Horror Show", the foundation for all that would follow, was a major success in

London, a failure on Broadway, and a success in Los Angeles. It has now been running practically continuously on stages around the world from 1973 to present.

The initially unsuccessful movie re-emerged as a midnight show blockbuster and has run continuously for 50 years. It has created what Hollywood calls a "waterfall"; "the industry's term not just for the dollars that a blockbuster can produce but for revenue that flows from the full complement of DVD, digital, rental and merchandising." And, in this case, a torrential, drenching down-pouring of soundtrack records and DVDs. (4)

The soundtrack that initially sold so poorly that the record company shelved it has now been reissued in twenty versions and became an indisputable money machine once "Rocky Horror" became a hit at midnight.

There were two failed attempts at building a linear connection to the movie's success: one by making a related movie ("Shock Treatment" in 1981) and the other ("Rocky Horror: Let's Do the Time Warp Again" in 2016) as a remake for a television special.

The ups and downs of the play, the movie, and the soundtrack, along with assorted "Rocky Horror" merchandise and books, round out the capitalization of Richard O'Brien's intellectual property. The triple crown of a half-century of box-office success, soundtrack sales, and stage play bookings, and the huge profits they have generated and the cash that continues to flow in, all revolve around the single action of taking "The Rocky Horror Picture Show" off the shelf at Fox and sending the failed movie into a new territory for Fox: the midnight show.

None of these successes would have happened without the rebirth of the movie as a midnight show, and the midnight show would not have happened without me, who did not like the movie but believed in it and fought for it at the studio when it was an orphan, and Alan Ladd, Jr., who believed in me and what I wanted to do with "The Rocky Horror Picture Show".

Laddie had emerged as the new president of the studio, and he personally intervened when I asked for his help after getting nowhere with my bosses. They had very actively resisted my plans to launch "Rocky Horror" as a midnight show.

He would become extremely successful as a studio head who delivered seventeen Academy Award nominated or winner movies to Fox in just a few years. Giving green lights for "Star Wars" and "The Rocky Horror Picture Show" at midnight were just two of his best decisions and successes.

Music would play a key role in the "Rocky Horror" experience. "The Rocky Horror Show: Original Roxy Cast" recording came out in 1974. The movie soundtrack, released in 1975, turned out to be, like the movie, a failure when first released but returned to life as a result of the midnight shows' successes.

"The soundtrack was the first thing in demand, by the midnight audience," said Sal Piro, president of the Rocky Horror Fan Club. (5)

The movie soundtrack for "Rocky Horror" was released by Lou Adler's Ode label to CBS (Epic) for retail sales on September 25, 1975, the day before "The Rocky Horror Picture Show" had its US premiere at the UA Westwood Theater.

But, with the box-office failure of the movie, the soundtrack "Was deleted everywhere but Canada," said Jem Records owner Marty Scott, who imported the soundtrack from CBS in Canada once the midnight show began. (6)

Adler questioned that, saying, "I terminated my deal with CBS - they no longer had the rights to my catalogue, including Canada." (7)

Scott recalls that, as the midnight show added bookings, "We had heard from stores across the country that there was a clamoring for the soundtrack to 'The Rocky Horror Picture Show.' We found out it was available from CBS Canada, a company with whom we had a great relationship. We started to import the album to great success. We couldn't keep it in stock. CBS had lost the US rights, and we went for it." (8)

"I contacted Lou Adler's office, where Marshall Blonstein was overseeing things for Ode, and cut a deal for JEM to manufacture and distribute 'The Rocky Horror Picture Show' soundtrack in America. Needless to say, it was an overnight sensation. An album that CBS (Epic) released and deleted was selling tens of thousands of copies. Then it was hundreds of thousands…we sold millions. 'The Rocky Horror Picture Show' was basically printing money". (9) Eventually, Adler's Ode Records would release over twenty versions of the soundtrack between 1975 and 2020. (10)

Another beneficiary of the midnight show's success was the stage play ("The Rocky Horror Show") that has run continuously around the world for a half-century. (11) Like the Frankenstein-ish character Rocky Horror (played by Peter Hinwood), the movie had arisen from the dead.

This book is the never-before-told story of how the midnight show happened, thanks (in addition to me and Laddie) to Bill Quigley, the Walter Reade Organization booker who gave me the initial playdate at the Waverly, Sal Piro, founder, and president of the Fan Club, and the very dedicated audiences at midnight. At every step of the way when I asked Lou Adler for his support, both with my plans for the movie and when it came to fact checking the galleys I shared with him, he readily agreed.

My studio colleagues seemed relieved with the shelving of the movie. Their heretofore arms-length relationship with the movie had been buffered by me and with no more theatrical life for it, their uneasiness was dissolved. I didn't notice that they ever had any opinion about Lou. If they had ever met him it was once during a release planning meeting. He was a recognized brand by then from his music successes, but his movie made them feel uncomfortable.

In the context of what was in production and being planned for production soon at Fox, which was just then collecting three of an eventual seventeen Oscar awards or nominations over the next couple of years, "The Rocky Horror Picture Show" was an anomaly in taste and content to what the studio was doing. It was also an inherited outside project and mostly unwelcome.

Although the movie did decent business for a while in Los Angeles, rationalizations were made by the studio that "of course, it would,"—there was a built-in audience and awareness because of the successful stage version at Adler's Roxy club—which is why the booking took place to begin with. The second booking, a college market flop in Columbus, Ohio (home of Ohio State University), seemed to question the college-kid booking strategy. Even though Austin, Texas, another college market, seemed to catch on, the movie was pulled from release.

The studio decided what to do about their concerns, and that was shared with me by my Fox bosses who told me to inform Adler. It was three-pointed: first, the movie was so far a financial loss of a half-million dollars, and a disappointment in a college market test where they had hopes of some success, so it was being written off on the studio's books. Next, with the bleak commercial prospects, the movie was being removed from release, and there would be no more bookings. Finally, as if there were a need for any more bad news, the Fox CEO was quoted about complaining that the "lips" marketing was "lewd and lascivious," and he wanted to distance the movie from the Fox name.

I called Lou and asked if I could come to see him, but did not say why. We met often, so it was not unusual to visit wherever he was: his nightclub (The Roxy), a Westwood office he shared with Robert Altman, Ode's office at A&M Records, his Bel Air mansion, and sometimes his Malibu beach retreat. He was then in Malibu, which gave me the time during a leisurely drive from the studio to the beach to think of what I was going to say, and not going say, to him.

It was definitely not going to be that the studio was pulling the plug on his movie. I knew that omission would cause me trouble with my bosses later, but right then, my goal was to engage Adler as an ally for what I wanted, which was a midnight show.

When I got to Malibu I withheld from Lou two of the three pieces of critical information that I was sent to deliver that were being used by Fox to pull the movie from release. I did not tell him that the studio considered it a financial loss, or that the CEO was against it. Lou would have already known about the failed college market test booking, but that's all.

Instead, I pitched him on going at midnight, using my experience at the NuArt Theater in West LA, where me and my friends would go at midnight on Fridays and Saturdays to hang out in the lobby and occasionally stick our heads into the auditorium to see John Water's "Pink Flamingos" (1972). I explained that it was like a "club" scene in a town that had almost no clubs that catered to college-aged kids. Madam Wong's in downtown LA, and later in

West LA, was a restaurant that morphed into a live music club was an exception.

Lou had been ahead of the pop culture curve for years, and this could be another way to stake out a place in the future. He liked the midnight idea which, for me, meant a chance of success for my plan because I intended to leverage his positive interest into a reversal of the shelving of the movie.

It also allowed me to shift the conversation from the negativity of why the studio lost faith in the movie into the positivity of breaking some new ground with a midnight release. That type of release was something no studio had ever done before.

As supple and agreeable as Lou was, which I really appreciated because his agreement gave me my ammo to use with my studio bosses, who were rigid to the point of petrification when it came to "Rocky Horror".

I knew there would be consequences when I returned to my bosses with the news that Lou liked my new plan, which was to go midnight, instead of reporting that he had accepted the shutting down of his movie. Just like never having shared with him that the original first-run booking strategy had been the "all queens" approach, I did not share with Lou that the studio was so dead set about shutting down "The Rocky Horror Picture Show". For me, it was a risk that I was willing to take: to go against my bosses by engaging Lou as a supporter of my plan.

I was very young and mostly unconcerned about the consequences if my bosses reacted badly.

My laid-back lifestyle living in free-spirited Topanga Canyon, where I was on the brink of relocating to its countercultural cousin Laurel Canyon, was an easy life, and I didn't let much bother me.

I had already interned for Stanley Kubrick on "2001: A Space Odyssey" (1968) as a teenager and had held manager-level studio executive jobs at both MGM and Fox by the time I was 23. I felt I had an established identity with good credentials and knew enough about the business to make me feel I could always work in the industry. At the worst, I could return to college for my senior year and get my diploma.

In my mind, I was anxious to launch a rescue mission like my MGM colleagues Mike Kaplan and Mike Shapiro had done with "2001:A Space Odyssey" when that Stanley Kubrick epic opened to poor reviews and bad box office. It had impressed me very much, as a teenager assisting Kubrick, to watch the dramatic turnaround in fortunes for "Space Odyssey", and I believed "Rocky Horror" was a candidate for the same type of reinvention.

But, now I was going up against my studio bosses, and I knew I would have no support, saving a miracle which later turned out to be new studio head (and Gordon Stulberg's replacement) Alan Ladd, Jr. But, that came later, after a lot of trouble, or maybe what could be called "good trouble."

I returned to the studio from my meeting with Lou, formulating my defense, which I felt may have to take the form of aggression, depending on the reaction of my bosses. I knew I had to be prepared for the worst.

Leaving Malibu, I drove south on the peaceful Pacific Coast Highway, glancing at the surfers in the rolling waves, cutting through Temescal Canyon to Sunset Boulevard, past the Will Rogers polo fields, and onto park-like San Vicente Boulevard with its usual joggers, I started to feel relaxed and confident that I could prevail after all.

While I felt I had already won the battle by getting Adler on my side, the real difficulty was how to help prevent the loss of face my bosses may feel if they had to turn 180 degrees on their plans to shelve the movie in order to accept my plan to go midnight. I intended to win, but I was also sensitive to the fact that I had to work with the very studio executives I was about to piss off. But, by now, I knew some of their vulnerabilities and intended to force them to blink, if I could.

"Never challenge someone's ego" was something Lou had told me early on. At the time, I thought it was code for how to deal with him. It came in useful in framing for me how to be ready to expect the worst reaction at Fox. My plan was to turn Lou's catchphrase around so that I would not be challenging my bosses' egos but counseling them not to challenge Lou's ego by not doing something he supported.

William Goldman, the Oscar-winning screenwriter for "Butch Cassidy and the Sundance Kid" (1969) and "All the President's Men" (1976), said that in Hollywood, "Nobody knows anything". (12) A good corollary to that is "act like you know something they don't," which I did. When I returned to the studio later in the day with Lou's approval of my plan to go midnight, my bosses immediately terminated me for doing the exact opposite of what they had told me to do. It was not unexpected by me.

I waited as they vented and then slowly laid out my defense to them, starting with the fact that when they made me the studio's point person with Lou Adler, they effectively nominated me as their designated agent and had reinforced that authority through the whole period the movie was being prepared for the opening commercial runs in Los Angeles and Columbus, Ohio by delegating practically all decision making to me, subject to their final approval. I claimed that their continued deference to me when it came to

"Rocky Horror" supported my authority. In proposing the midnight show to the producer, I felt I was acting appropriately in my role, and had the best interest of obtaining profits for the studio in mind.

When I left Fox to go to Malibu I told them I had no plan for a midnight show. As I drove the very slow and scenic route was when I developed it, I explained. Had I known my plan before I left the studio, I told my bosses I would have obviously shared it with them but, I suggested that inspiration has no set boundaries: when it hits can be very unpredictable.

That was not true. I had my plan worked out and knew I'd be in a stronger position if I secured interest from the producer first before pitching midnight to my bosses and risking them saying no.

For me, it was taking "Rocky Horror" to midnight or accepting that it was dead. Home video had not been introduced yet, and cable was minimal. The only "ancillary" market for movies was 16mm bookings at schools and other institutions. A long shot could have been going through Films, Inc., the major 16mm, non-theatrical distributor that might help find a college audience for the movie. Schools and institutions were required to get a license to show movies, and companies like Films Inc., which was "by far the biggest, and most important of all…known as the 'Tiffany' of 16mm distributors". (13) But, making it an even longer long shot, the college market test for the movie had already failed, with Austin, Texas, being a notable exception.

Going midnight, a format I knew from my late nights on weekends at the NuArt, was the only alternative that interested me.

As I explained the idea of going midnight to my bosses, I told them that I had made a representation to the producer that the studio would take the movie into the midnight market, even though there was no studio knowledge of this or commitment yet, and that I had obtained approval from the producer for that action. I reminded them many times in meetings where they talked about how to be sure they were marketing and distributing movies in a bulletproof way to avoid being sued by producers who may become unhappy with what they did. Like doctors with malpractice worries, studios had maldistribution worries. The default defense was always, "This is what the producer agreed to".

So, this—a midnight platform—"is what the producer agreed to," was backed up with a reminder to them that Lou Adler and Michael White could sue Fox for maldistribution if they failed to go through with it in at least one-midnight market, to get a sense of its viability. I pointed out that all I was really asking them to understand was that this was a stay of execution: to delay their yanking the movie out of release until every possibility for success had been attempted.

I told them they would be challenging Adler's ego about what he thought was good for his movie if they said "No". Finally,if they were killing my plan, I asked them to get on the speaker phone while we were all together and call Lou so they could tell him the bad news. Instead, they cancelled my termination and approved one test market at midnight in what they called a "minor market". Later that afternoon, I called Lou from my office and told him how happy Fox was that he endorsed the midnight show concept. There was an important result of this brinkmanship. It created huge and unexpected windfall profits.

I immediately took control of "Rocky Horror" marketing and distribution from then on. Nobody else wanted anything to do with the movie and I simply filled a vacuum. My bosses reluctantly gave me their approval to "test" my midnight show concept in one "minor" market.

Everything that would follow for "Rocky Horror" for the next fifty years turned on the decision to take the movie off the shelf and send it into the midnight marketplace.

Instead of "The Rocky Horror Picture Show" and collaterally "The Rocky Horror Picture Show" soundtrack album and CDs being failed and forgotten has-beens, they would become winners that brought in tens of millions of dollars to the profit participants, created hundreds of thousands of fans, and made movie history.

I knew my bosses were under duress from me when they agreed to let me explore my midnight plans and I did not want to push them any more than necessary. Despite having this as my own discrete project, I still had to work collaboratively with everyone on the marketing and sales teams on other projects at the studio.

These included some of the biggest movies that Fox was then releasing, such as "Young Frankenstein" (1974), "Silent Movie" (1976), "The Omen" (1976), "Star Wars" (1977), "Julia" (1977), "The Turning Point" (1977), and "High Anxiety" (1977).

As long as I tried to fit in as a team player, all was fine, but I always felt an underlying tension like a bubble was about to burst. That's what happened when I took my next step, which was to identify a market and a theater for the first-midnight show.

Los Angeles was out of consideration because the movie had already played and failed there, and I had been told not to go to a big city. Looking around at where there were any good art houses that were playing midnight shows, I found the Waverly theater in New York City that was then playing Alejandro Jodorowsky's "El Topo" (1970), a movie noted for its non-stop shocking moments. I learned that the Walter Reade Organization's Waverly had a reputation for midnight shows and had run some of the best indie films in that slot. Movies like "El Topo" (1970) "The Night of the

Living Dead" (1968), "The Harder They Come" (1972), and "Pink Flamingos" (1972).

While I was trying to figure out what to do with the then-shelved "The Rocky Horror Picture Show", Fox was making plans for how it would handle its slate of mainstream movies scheduled for release. In 1976, the year "The Rocky Horror Picture Show" would have its first midnight show, Fox was firmly into the Laddie regime of moviemaking. Among the twenty-six titles slated for release that year were Mel Brook's "Silent Movie", Paul Mazursky's "Next Stop Greenwich Village", and Richard Donner's "The Omen", all having been green-lighted by Laddie.

To share the exciting news with exhibitors and press from around the country, Fox hosted a massive gala event in early January called, "26 for 76" on one of the studio's biggest sound stages. It was both a pitch and a party. Seated on the triple dais were stars and celebrities, moviemakers and studio executives. Each of us on staff working that night was assigned to shadow a VIP.

The business purpose of the party was to get exhibitors to "blind bid" on the upcoming movies. On the Monday following the party, Fox sales managers from around the country would be calling them and asking them to sign exhibition contacts for the movies they had seen clips from at the party. That's what made the bidding blind: the theater owners had to contract for the 26 movies without ever having seen anything more than a promo clip. Blind bidding and its cousin, block booking, would be outlawed just a few years later.

One of the significant movies showcased at the party was "Star Wars". Although slated for 1977 release, the hope was that exhibitors would contract for it based on only seeing a poster. No clips were available. The movie had not yet started filming;

principal photography began on March 22, 1976. The teaser poster was simple and carried the slogan "A boy, a girl, and a universe".

In the audience that night was Bill Quigley, a young theater booker for the Walter Reade Organization. The WRO theaters in New York City were some of the most sought-after venues for movies, and Bill would have been at "26 for 76" as an interested buyer and booker.

I did not know Bill or anyone at WRO, but WRO's The Waverly was on my mind as a likely venue for taking "Rocky Horror" to midnight release, so I reached out to Bill in a phone call, requesting a meeting with him the next time I was in New York.

A few weeks after "26 for 76", I flew to New York and met with Quigley at his office and pitched him to play "Rocky Horror" at midnight, and he said yes. The Waverly was already playing midnight shows, so he knew that side of the business. He agreed to an early April release and said he would hold it for a few weekends to let it build an audience.

Bill was already playing midnight shows—which was what drew me to WRO—and my outreach to him resulted in the Waverly becoming the first theatre in the country to play a midnight show of "The Rocky Horror Picture Show".

Quigley knew the midnight market well and, as an exhibitor, actively engaged in playing offbeat movies at midnight on weekends. He later recalled that "Midnight shows were a great way of generating incremental income for the theaters. You're operating 365 days a year, and you have a high fixed cost. 80-90 percent of the business was on the weekend. At the Waverly it became a question of "How can we generate incremental revenue to drop to the bottom line?" There was a very light operating cost in running the midnight shows". (14)

Once the Quigley meeting had been set, I turned my attention to job protection. I knew I had to be prepared for failure and possible termination at Fox, so I made a "plan B" for my continued employment.

A friend of mine worked at Paramount Pictures, then headquartered in New York, so I called him and asked if he would be able to get me an introductory meeting with his boss, telling him I had been the MGM Foreign Publicity Manager and was now the Fox Advertising Manager, and was interested in working for Paramount. It was surprisingly easy: he called back the next day and said just let them know when I wanted to stop by.

What I was hoping for, and got when the interview went well, was an offer for a job at Paramount, specifically a sales department executive position in one of their branch offices. I knew publicity and advertising from my MGM and Fox jobs respectively. Rounding that out with some sales experience at Paramount would add value to my resume. I was afraid Fox would not like that I was attempting to book a midnight show in New York, the biggest movie market in America. Now, I had another job, just in case I needed to move studios.

After my Paramount meeting, I went to see Bill Quigley at WRO and returned to Los Angeles later that day with a Paramount job in my back pocket, and a Waverly booking contract in my jacket pocket.

Before leaving New York, I called Lou to give him the good news about the Waverly. I wanted to wait and tell my bosses in person. I had taken a sick day and booked my air ticket privately, not through the studio's travel desk; they had no idea I was even in New York. I knew I had to be prepared for a negative reaction when I returned to the studio.

Back in Los Angeles, I brought the exhibition agreement with Walter Reade to Peter Myers, the vice president of sales, and asked him to sign it. An hour later, I was terminated for the second time, this time for booking a playdate in New York instead of a "minor" market. Once again, I fought back. I wanted the Waverly and used my leverage of saying, "Call Lou and tell him that yourself, that Fox won't sign a booking contract for the Waverly for a playdate that Lou liked". Having him be unhappy with them and me hinting at them of litigation, something Lou never expressed to me, was something I found effective in dealings with my bosses. Their fear of Lou being unhappy with what they were doing with his movie was a vulnerability I had identified and happily exploited.

The two biggest stumbling blocks to my plans for taking "Rocky Horror" to midnight were Jonas Rosenfield and Peter Myers. Rosenfield, my big boss, was VP of advertising and publicity, and Myers was VP of sales. Between them, they had already fired me twice over "Rocky Horror". They were in total control of Fox's marketing and distribution of movies. Nothing happened without their personal approval. On my side, all I had was persistence.

Neither executive had the slightest interest in "The Rocky Horror Picture Show," and that trickled down to their teams that similarly ignored me or put up barriers to what I wanted to do. I was even given a time management analysis that questioned if I was wasting time on "Rocky Horror" when I should be working on other movies.

I kept the Waverly's booking contact in my suit jacket pocket at all times and every time I was with Myers, which was at least weekly for marketing meetings, but sometimes just passing him in the hallways, I'd pull it out and ask him to sign it. Each time, he refused.

Finally, I stood in his office doorway early one morning, waiting for him to come to work, and blocked his entry. I offered him an alternative: call security to make me move or sign the contract. He signed, but said that he and Jonas had already decided that I'd be fired the day the movie opened. I already knew that from Jonas.

To his credit, once Myers saw the Waverly results he softened and eventually told his sales team that no bookings were to be made without my agreement. While he was stubborn in the beginning, he became very pragmatic when he saw strong box office results. He survived Laddie's purge. Jonas Rosenfield did not.

The opening was set for midnight on Friday, April 2, 1976. My marketing concept for launching the midnight show at the Waverly was based on a single word: "discovery", meaning that you would fall into the theater not knowing too much about what to expect, be surprised, and liked it enough to tell friends and spread word of mouth about what you had "discovered". Unlike traditional movie openings—and how we did it with the Los Angeles first-run engagement of "Rocky Horror"—there would be no paid advertising, and no studio-generated publicity push, press screenings, or interviews by the cast. I reached out to Tim Curry to let him know the strategy and asked that he not engage in any publicity. I think Tim was possibly feeling like he would never get out the identification as Dr. Frank N. Furter, and may have been happy not to have to keep perpetuating that persona in press interviews.

For the Waverly, I only used a trailer on the screen and some small flyers handed out in and around the theater. Walter Reade and Fox shared the cost for a very small directory ad in the Village Voice to announce the midnight show. The studio gave me $75,000 ($350,000 today) for advertising, which was a decent budget. I wound up spending $65 ($304 today) to open "Rocky Horror" at the Waverly. A few days before opening, the advertising vice president at Fox, my big boss Jonas Rosenfield, asked to see my budget and was shocked to see how minimalist it was. My immediate boss, advertising director Steve Panama, was spending time on special assignments in Tokyo and Australia, which meant there was no buffer between me and what would become a very angry Rosenfield when he learned that I had not spent the $75,000 he allocated to me to open the movie. Jonas wanted to know why there was no large ad in the New York Times. I explained my discovery concept to him. I had become so independent in my operations, and with Steve away during this period, that I was not looping in any other staff to my plans, so Rosenfield had no idea what I was doing. I successfully resisted his attempt to advertise in the New York Times by dragging my feet and not giving the ad agency enough time to place it in the paper in time for the movie's opening night. Once again, I conjured my lifeline to maintain the integrity of my program: the image of a possibly litigious Lou Adler. All Jonas could do was remind me I was going to be fired after the movie opened.

Now, it was do or die time for the movie: opening night. If the movie did even fair business, I knew I had a chance because Bill Quigley had promised to let it run for a few weekends to find an audience. But, if nobody showed up, I knew the threatened termination would probably take place on Monday. So, on what could have been the beginning of the end for me, I told my girlfriend Margie Doppelt that I wanted to get out of town for the weekend to either Santa Barbara or Palm Springs, both of which were an easy drive from Los Angeles. Santa Barbara was the site of the disastrous sneak preview. I was hoping that I would hear better news if I were in Palm Springs, so she and I went to the desert resort to wait out the opening weekend at the Waverly.

A few days earlier, I asked Bill Quigley for the private number of the manager at the Waverly and then called Denise Borden to say I was anxious to know how we were doing, and could I call her for a box office gross late Friday night (Los Angeles time). Denise said to call around 1 am (Eastern time), and when I did, she said there was nothing to worry about.... the show had sold out. I called again the next night and got the same reply. On Monday, Quigley confirmed how happy Walter Reade was with the opening.

At the weekly Fox marketing meeting on the Monday after the Waverly opening, where the sales and marketing teams reviewed all Fox weekend grosses and new openings (like "Rocky Horror"), nobody said anything to me about the midnight opening. However, the Hollywood exhibition and distribution community is very small, and word gets out quickly when there's a movie that does well.

One of the Fox division sales managers had called that morning and asked for a midnight booking for the Dobie Theater in Austin, Texas. That was a great sign: Austin was a vibrant college market as the home of the University of Texas-Austin. The Varsity Theater in Austin had played a regular engagement before the movie was yanked by the studio, and they were anxious to "go midnight". I supported the booking request. Austin would be a revealing playdate that would show if the movie could hit a midnight audience of college kids, which it did right from the start of the engagement.

Later in the day, Laddie called me to say congratulations. I mentioned I was told today was my last day at Fox. He said no, there's going to be some changes, and I want you on my team. Very shortly after that, he purged the old team and elevated a new one that included me, along with a promotion to worldwide advertising director.

With the bookings beginning to be set and successful, I created the simple business plan of no studio spending on advertising for the movie and supported how Bill Quigley wanted the theatrical revenue to be split with the exhibitors. This became the model for

Fox branch offices to use when they booked midnight shows of "Rocky Horror".

Seeing how successful a minimal advertising campaign was to open the Waverly, I got studio and producer approval not to spend any money, but to let the movie be "discovered" by audiences and let word of mouth do the promoting of the midnight show. The Waverly opening was supported by $65 in paid advertising by the studio and a small ad in the Village Voice. That tiny media buy was supplemented by a poster and a trailer at the theater and some handbill-sized flyers at the theater. That became the successful "discovery marketing plan" for other midnight bookings.

Bill Quigley's film rental formula was accepted and used by Fox everywhere. "I made the 'template' deal with Fox for how to split box office revenues on 'The Rocky Horror Picture Show,' and it's a formula that a senior distribution executive friend of mine has said is the standard 'Rocky Horror' licensing deal for midnight shows around the country, and always has been. Originally, Fox wanted a 90/10 deal, meaning they got 90%. I negotiated at 80/20 to give theaters more revenue." (15)

Once the studio received their film rental and took a reduced distribution fee off the top, which was 20% (not the usual 35%) when I was at Fox, and with no need to deduct advertising costs, the result became the profits to share between the profit participants Fox and Adler and any subsidiary right holders. Record and CD sales, home video and DVDs, and merchandise licensing all had their own profit splits.

Lou Adler and Michale White's initial $1,300,000 cost to make the movie paid off, thanks to the engine of the midnight show, in one of the greatest returns on investment for any movie except those in the mega-blockbuster profitability range like "Star Wars". This was setting another record to go along with being the longest continuously running movie in history: the record for nearly unmatchable profitability.

Other accolades that followed with "Rocky Horror" rising from the dead included it becoming one of "The 10 most successful R-rated movies ever" (16), and one of the "10 Best R-Rated Movie Musicals, Ranked By IMDb". (17)

When the movie transitioned to midnight, the "don't dream it be it" theme was the first time that Hollywood reached out so directly and specifically to the LGBT community. It was a clarion call on a par with MGM selling "2001: A Space Odyssey" a few years earlier as "the ultimate trip", knowing how effective the use of coded language in advertising would be for reaching a druggie audience that was mesmerized by the incredible light show toward the end of the movie. The use of Richard O'Brien's "don't dream it, be it" lyrical phrase was similarly directed to reach the midnight audience with a sentiment they would recognize.

The movie was "very attractive to the gay audience" when it opened, says Fan Club President Sal Piro, and continued to attract gays as well as straights. (18) "The audience became more straight as the years went on. Men were dressing as Dr. Frank 'N Furter, in fishnets, a corset and heels and turning their girlfriends on." (19)

The embracement by a fluid audience earned the movie a place as the number three "Queer Cinema Essentials For Everyone to Watch" (20) and recognition as one of the "Top 10 Groundbreaking Queer Films" (21)

I was disappointed that Lou Adler did not leverage his "Rocky Horror" success at Fox into more movies for the studio. He seemed to be wanting to transition from records to film and already had a couple of movies to his credit: "Monterey Pop" (1968) and

"Brewster McCloud" (1970). He and Laddie would have been a powerful combination. Lou had a proven track record during the '50s, 60's, and early 70's for what was emerging in pop culture, and Laddie knew how to make high-quality, award-worthy movies.

As "Rocky Horror" spread out across the country, David Lynch, who I had met through a mutual friend at Fox Stuart Cornfeld when we were both working on a Mel Brooks movie, asked if I would ask Fox to release some of the midnight theater time slots where "Rocky Horror" was playing, so he could play what was becoming his indie cult movie "Eraserhead" (1978) at midnight.

Stuart had arranged for Lynch to screen the movie for me at Fox, and I liked it. I was looking for more indie movies that would fit into the midnight market to build Fox's catalog. Unfortunately, "Eraserhead" already had a distributor, Libra, and Fox could not be a sub-distributor for them. But, I told David that in the long run other studios, where he might have his next movie, would benefit from my pathfinding. Today, playing at midnight is routine for all studios. It's a solid market slot.

The five million dollar lifetime box-office gross that I had predicted to Laddie was now looking realistic, with Austin and New York causing enough success to attract other theaters around the country for midnight bookings. The requests for playdates and prints came flowing into Fox, and managing "Rocky Horror" to get it firmly established became my number one priority.

Soon, Fox owned the midnight market and had secured all the best art houses and college market venues to play "Rocky Horror" at midnight. The track swelled to about 250 theaters nationwide.

The formulas for marketing using very low-key messaging (mainly trailers and flyers) and film rental splits were working nicely and were applied to the markets and theaters I liked. Most important was a decision, that Lou agreed to, that Fox would not spend any advertising money on "Rocky Horror" but just let it grow by a word-of-mouth reputation.

It was courageous for Lou to agree to that. Most producers are the opposite: they want a studio to spend a fortune on advertising. But for Lou, less cost meant he got more profit. For me, no advertising meant my "discovery" concept was being validated.

Everything at Fox having to do with "Rocky Horror" now needed my sign-off, and the sales and marketing staffs came to respect me for my work that brought revenues to their program. As the movie established its successful midnight journey, I asked Laddie not to look at me anymore as a studio employee but as a revenue producer and to treat me that way. I knew my value to him and Fox, and directly expressed that to him.

Studio CEO Dennis Stanfill, who had once called the marketing of "Rocky Horror Picture Show" "lewd and lascivious" praised "Rocky Horror" alongside "Star Wars" as examples of important and successful movies for the studio. (22)

Ultimately Laddie, with Stanfill's approval, made sure that I was rewarded with a raise and a bonus, a bigger, newly decorated office, rare curbside parking, a promotion to worldwide advertising director, and awarded stock options, but it would not officially be for "Rocky Horror". I had met with Stanfill privately and asked him for one percent of the studio's gross on "Rocky Horror". As happy as he was with "Rocky Horror's" bottom line, I think he was still embarrassed by the movie. He shifted the recognition for my work by putting me in the very exclusive executive bonus plan for helping to successfully market "Star Wars", another release I had worked intimately on.

I continued to work on the wave of midnight bookings that was being set up, and stayed at Fox until Laddie quit to go to Warner Brothers, with his new Ladd Company, to make movies with them after having a fallout with Stanfill. I opened a marketing business with Mel Brooks and Francis Ford Coppola as my first two clients and, 15 years later, a Steven Spielberg project with the United Nations as my last client.

I kept in touch occasionally with Lou and Sal Piro over the years, especially at the tenth and fifteenth anniversaries of the Waverly opening.

Over the decades, "The Rocky Horror Picture Show" movie and soundtrack records and CDs continued to be solid gold annuities.

Half a century ago, nobody would think that a dead "Rocky Horror" would transform like Frankenstein (or the movie character Rocky Horror) and come back from the dead and have such a long life.

The international market for "Rocky Horror" responded more to the stage play than the movie. While the play has been in continuous performance around the world since 1973 (23) the movie has not delivered the level of international results as in the domestic market.

Movies make money all around the world, unless there are

built-in constraints. Fox had already experienced failure with "The Rocky Horror Picture Show" in the United States except for a very narrow audience segment that came out at midnight. But, from that acceptance, the studio knew it had something to build on, if only it could be replicated in foreign territories.

If the movie was successful, maybe the music would be also, and then the merchandising. That was the three-legged stool of "Rocky Horror" profitability: success at midnight theaters, success with the soundtrack, and success with spin-off merchandising. But, the primary leg of the stool was the movie playing in a theater at midnight in an environment of fan experience.

"We had problems throughout international markets" recalled Jean-Louis Rubin, then the Vice President of 20th Century Fox International. (24) "The notion of midnight shows did not work. The concept was totally alien. In the United States midnight was popular, but not in Europe." (25) "We just couldn't make it work. We tried press screenings, but the press didn't follow up. Or show any interest in the movie. There were no weekly magazines catering to the film audience. Maybe now would be the time to try to bring it back. The film has not been dated, but it's now owned by Disney." (26)

"There was a question of why it didn't do well in England. The play started there and was successful, but it didn't translate into a movie. However, in southern Germany, Bavaria was a big success. It ran in a tiny theater (50-60 seats) for a long time. It did fine there as a midnight show. However, that was unique to that part of Germany". (27)

Perhaps, I suggested to Rubin, it was successful there because Bavaria was the ancestral home of Ludwig, the "mad king" of Bavaria, and there was an easier acceptance of the movie and it's theme of "don't dream it be it" which certainly described Ludwig's lifestyle depicted in history, and on the big screen by Luchino Visconti who was one of the great film directors of larger than life, operatic stories such as "The Leopard" (1963), and "The Damned" (1969). He told Ludwig's story, rife with fantastical castles such as the legendary Neuschwanstein, grandiose dreams and ambitions, and a screened gay lifestyle in "Ludwig: The Mad King of Bavaria" (1973) that may have touched a Bavarian nerve that resonated with "Rocky Horror" and made finding an audience to sustain a midnight show in Bavaria easier than in other international territories. Ludwig had a reputation. He did not just dream it; he was it.

On the other side of the world, in Tokyo, the opposite reception greeted attempts to book "Rocky Horror". "Any subject that catered to the gay community was a big taboo" said Rubin. (28)

That was not all. "The problem in Japan was that Japan is a buyers market—you play a circuit A or B and you are locked in with your client. You have no alternative. It was either Toho Cinemas, Japan's largest film exhibitor, or the Shochiku group. There's very little flexibility. Fox played exclusively with Toho. The concept of having a small art theater for a long run didn't exist. There was definitely a lack of theaters to begin with." (29).

"We were faced with those problems relevant to the market. A main issue is that in a country where you must subtitle not dub, the moment you have music attached it looses the market. Even in dubbing territories, it's impossible to dub musicals. How do you do that? You lose so much stuff." (30)

Lou Adler had a different experience with the movie in Japan; he saw a street-level scene of success. "I think the Tokyo government had something to do with not getting a theatre to stay with it" he told me. "It was a street success. I evidenced that on my trips there, at gatherings like on Saturday at Harajuku, which is a renowned center of Japanese youth culture and fashion. And the merch" continued Lou, "we have a terrific poster. And the music—at the 25th Anniversary in LA we flew in a Japanese cover band." (31)

"I do remember some street activities in the Shinjiku district in Tokyo where the gay community would get together kind of underground movement; the travesty aspect was a big part of it - may be in the culture: Kabuki, No - the person behind the mask", recalled Rubin. (32)

Despite these bright spots, Rubin concluded that, "The life of 'Rocky Horror' in foreign was not very good". (33)

Being locked out of the foreign theatrical market has not hindered the runaway success in the domestic market. As the world shrinks, and Marshall McLuhan's "global village" expands, there is a chance for worldwide growth of "The Rocky Horror Picture Show". Not so much by in-theater shows at midnight, but through the "Rocky Horror" fandom cyber communities that connect our shrinking world. There is no reason why "Rocky Horror" can not become a global brand. The play is already well-known in many international markets. People are being it, not dreaming it, all over the world.

"Hollywood didn't know what to do with 'The Rocky Horror Picture Show', said author Vito Russo. (34) But he was wrong: I was a Hollywood studio executive, and I did know exactly what to do.

Maybe the younger Adler generation, now in their 20's and 30's, of Manny, Ike, Oscar and Pablo will be the next ones to figure out what to do with this Adler legacy and continue to grow its fandom to the next level: a global audience that already devours American pop culture.

As the movie celebrates its 50th anniversary, a whole new generation of fans is available worldwide. Like the Roxy nightclub that their older brothers Nicholai and Cisco operate with their dad, "The Rocky Horror Picture Show" profits help sustain the Adler family.

Notes:

1. Time Magazine, 5/21/73

2. https://variety.com/2015/film/news/rocky-horror-picture-show-at-40-40th-anniversary-1201600333/

3. https://www.nytimes.com/2020/12/02/movies/godfather-coda-francis-ford-coppola.html

4. https://www.washingtonpost.com/business/2020/12/09/warner-hbo-move-angers-hollywood/

5. interview with author 11/26/19

6. https://theseconddisc.com/2013/07/31/interview-excavating-jem-with-marty-scott/

7. to author 5/22/20

8. https://theseconddisc.com/2013/07/31/interview-excavating-jem-with-marty-scott/

9. ibid

10. http://www.rockyhorrorwiki.org/wiki2/index.php?title=The_Rocky_Horror_Picture_Show_Original_Soundtrack_Album

11. https://en.wikipedia.org/wiki/The_Rocky_Horror_Show

12. https://variety.com/2018/film/opinion/william-goldman-dies-appreciation-1203030781/

13. https://kitparkerfilms.wordpress.com/tag/16mm-non-theatrical/

14. interview with author 8/29/19

15. interview with author 7/29/19

16. https://www.businessinsider.com/highest-grossing-r-rated-films-of-all-time-2016-7

17. https://screenrant.com/best-adult-r-rated-movie-musicals-ranked-imdb-score/

18. interview with author 5/23/19

19. ibid

20. https://www.themanual.com/culture/10-best-queer-films/

21. source:https://www.wescreenplay.com/blog/top-10-groundbreaking-queer-films/).

22. Stanfill to executives

23. https://en.wikipedia.org/wiki/The_Rocky_Horror_Show

24. interview with author 5/18/20)

25. ibid

26. ibid

27. ibid

28. ibid

29. ibid

30. ibid

31. to author 5/19/20

32. to author 5/18/20

33. ibid

34. Vito Russo - "The Celluloid Closet", pp.52-53, Harper and Row Publishers, New York 1981

Chapter 9
Those Lips - Building A Brand

Five stories behind the iconic "Rocky Horror" lips.

As powerful an image as Tim Curry's entry is, descending in the elevator belting out the tune "Sweet Transvestite", the iconic image for "The Rocky Horror Picture Show" is "those lips" that were used in three iterations: over the opening of the movie, in the trailer, and on the poster. Whose lips they are, and the stories behind them about how it happened, is a little known insight of how the "Rocky Horror" lips brand that became so famous was created.

A pair of lips has triggered sensuality for centuries. Lipsticked red lips only enhance the attraction. The cigarette company, "Philip Morris," knew that lips were a part of women's vocabulary of sensualness. In 1920, they introduced Marlboro, as an extremely mild cigarette aimed at women smokers that featured the advertising tag line "Mild As May", and a red tip that helped to mask lip-stick traces.

In 1954, Chicago ad agency 'Leo Burnett Company repackaged Marlboro as a "Man's" cigarette, featuring a cowboy in its advertising. They kept the color red as the identity that had been built into their branding from day one as a woman's smoke. (1)

It is no surprise that a 2010 study by Manchester University's lead scientist, Dr. Geoff Beattie, suggests that, "red lips perceive attractiveness and are still inextricably linked, with red lipstick; the most powerful attractor, that significantly increases visual fixation". (2)

The "Rocky Horror" lips sing, they sell, and they seduce in the movie's opening, the trailer, and the poster, respectively.

I was able to interview Tony Seiniger, whose agency Seiniger Advertising created the famous "lips" poster, and also interviewed Lorelei Shark, whose lips those are. I also interviewed Jeff Kanew, who created the trailer, and Rhea Ruggiero, whose lips were used in it. However, Patricia Quinn (Magenta) provided her lips over the opening song of the movie.

Those Lips That Open the Movie:

Patricia Quinn's lips were used in the song, "Science Fiction/Double Feature" and Richard O'Brien sang the song, in the opening scene of "The Rocky Horror Picture Show." The duo of Patricia Quinn (lips and Magenta in the film) and Richard O'Brien (Riff Raff) were a perfect pair.

In what could have been a lost-lips-sinks-cinema moment, Quinn nearly bolted when she learned that she would not be singing the "Science Fiction/Double Feature" song that opened the movie. She was essentially reprising her stage play role as the cigarette girl who sings the tune to open the play.

Quinn was ready to go... "I said to them, 'So I'm not singing Science Fiction? because that's the only reason I took the part in the first place, not for Magenta, but for that song. The usherette sings that, and then I become Magenta..she doubled up...They said, "No, it won't work...

so I said, "Well, I'm sorry then, I don't want to do this film".

(3)

In the end, Quinn was featured as the lips mouthing the words to "Science Fiction/Double Feature" that was sung, using his voice, by Richard O'Brien.

Those Lips Last Forever on the Poster (4)

An interview with poster designer Tony Seiniger

TD - What inspired you to shift gears in the "look" for the advertising campaign (creating the key art that would be used in the poster and newspaper ads) when the successful stage play of "The Rocky Horror Show" already had an established "look" for how they we're selling the play? Why wasn't that good enough for the movie?

TS - We did use the play's logo, and the dripping blood typeface. But I wanted to create something that was sexier and a bit kinky, hence the biting lips. The play's image, if I remember it correctly, it was more of a horror image, and I felt that might limit the audience and the film's appeal. Besides, I was being directed by Jonas to come up with something new.

TD - Can you give a little background to hearing the Fox vice president of advertising and publicity, Jonas Rosenfield, confiding to you that "We don't know what to do with this," and you told him, "Why don't we just have some fun?"

TS - When I was assigned "The Rocky Horror Picture Show," Jonas admitted that he had no idea of what the campaign should look like. He said it might be a question of generation gap, that this movie was not intended for his age group, but was something for "the kids." He was unable to give me any creative direction, and left it up to me to do what I thought would be the right look for the movie.

TD - What was your first step in the process of creating the poster?

TS - As I always tried to do, I came up with that simple, strong graphic. I would have left the campaign to the lips poster, but Jonas asked for a more "traditional" look as well. He said the lips were fine for a teaser poster, but he wanted a real one sheet, too. That's why the yellow poster exists. It's never been one of my favorites.

TD -- In the mid 1970's, when "Rocky Horror" was released in theaters, the pop culture environment was radically changing. Moviegoer tastes were moving away from "Sound of Music" towards "Bonnie and Clyde," and music was advancing from folk and teeny-bopper music to harder-edged rock and roll; and eventually to psychedelic music. Was there a similar paradigm shift in the graphic arts and creative advertising world that you were at the center of?

TS -— Beginning in the early 60s, advertising went through a major revolution. The era of accounts being controlled by account executives, as portrayed in "Mad Men," was ending, and the creatives (art directors and copywriters) were becoming the real stars on Madison Avenue. Agencies like Doyle Dane Bernbach were leading the revolution. Illustration, which had been the predominant visual technique, was being replaced by photography. Advertising design became simple, clean, and graphic. Think of those Volkswagen billboards.

The change in movie poster design was a reaction to what was being created on Madison Avenue. I believe the first really radically different movie campaign was "Rosemary's Baby" (1968). The campaign was directed by Steve Frankfurt, then president and creative director of Young & Rubicam, a very successful and large agency, that, like Doyle Dane, was pushing advertising into more and more creative solutions. The poster was designed by Phil Gips. We at EUE shot the TV spots, which were basically audio/visual versions of the poster.

The copy line "Pray for Rosemary's Baby" was written by Steve Gordon, who was at Y & R at the time. Steve went on to direct more movie campaigns while still running Y&R. "Goodbye Columbus," "Catch 22," and "Alien," to mention just a few.

I left EUE in 1968 and formed a small agency called The Madison Experience. My partner, Dick Hanley, had been a copywriter at J. Walter Thompson. We worked for every major film distributor that was headquartered in New York. Photography was my minor in art school, and I always tried to bring that sensibility to our work. Throughout my career I made a point of seeking out and hiring the best photographers available.

TD - What's the history of the "A Different Set of Jaws," slogan for the poster that ranks with "The Ultimate Trip," for "2001: A Space Odyssey" (1968), "Just When You Thought It Was Safe To Go Back in The Water" for "Jaws" (1975), and "In Space, Nobody Can Hear You Scream" for "Alien" (1979) as iconic messaging.? Did you write that line?

TS - Yes. I wrote that line. I worked on the "Jaws" campaign soon after starting Seiniger Advertising. That poster did more for helping to build the agency than anything else. After I came up with the biting lip visual, the copy line seemed to write itself; I guess more of an homage to the "Jaws" poster as anything else.

TD - What do you think about the fact that your "lips" and "a different set of jaws" poster has become the longest continuously used poster to advertise the longest continuously running movie (50 years and still playing) in history? Did you ever think you would be making advertising history with this piece of work?

TS - You, my friend, are largely responsible for the phenomenon that "The Rocky Horror Picture Show" has become. The lips poster survives because of what you created. It's a strong, simple graphic, and designs like that are timeless.

Meet Lorelei - those lips on the poster (5)

Interview with Lorelei Shark, whose lips were featured on the poster.

TD - How were you picked to be the lips for the poster for "The Rocky Horror Picture Show"?

LS - I was a pretty well-known model, specializing in eyes, lips, and hair, so a photographer I knew from other jobs hired me.

TD - What was it about your lips that you think got you the job?

LS - I was actually known for my pout! Pouting gives lips a fuller appearance. It's what all the models do today, but I was the only one who did it in the late 60s and early 70s. My very first modeling job was focused on my lips. It was for KISS radio in Los Angeles. They were used on billboards in 1969 to promote KISS Radio. That led to lipstick commercials and, eventually, to "The Rocky Horror Picture Show" poster using my lips.

TD - What was the "Rocky Horror" shoot like?

LS - It took about two hours. The photographer kept saying, "pull up harder, pull up harder," to get the image of me biting my lips.

TD - How did you become a model with such specialization?

LS - The circumstances were that I needed work. I was about to go to work as a waitress at a sports bar called 'The Point After,' but my very good friend Janice Pennington, who was the most beautiful girl I ever saw, said, "Grab some pictures" of you and come with me to an open casting call for Playboy After Dark." The television show was hosted by Hugh Hefner, and set in a party scene where Hefner interviewed celebrity guests. I was asked if I could dance, and when the auditions were over both Janice and I got hired for what would be the last season.

I was hired for Playboy for years, for men's clothing spreads and what sort of man reads Playboy, but I never got undressed because I didn't want my kids to see me that way.

I never thought I'd be a model, but I discovered being small could be an advantage. I was able to make cars and furniture look larger.

My features and hair became what most clients sought, ; my specialties became lips, eyes, teeth, and hair.

Those Lips Star in the Trailer (6)

I interviewed Jeff Kanew, the trailer maker, and Rhea Ruggiero, the lips model in the trailer.

TD - Your "Rocky Horror" trailer hit many nerves; here's what Lisa Sutton, a fan, told me. "I grew up in Los Angeles, and my first exposure to 'The Rocky Horror Picture Show' was when I saw the trailer at the UA Westwood before it opened. I was at a movie with my father, who must have seen my eyes pop out of my head as the trailer played, because he leaned in to me and said, 'I'm NOT taking you to see THAT!' That made me decide, now I have to see it...I managed to make it on my own a few hundred times over the next few years. It was electric, and struck me the moment I saw the trailer".

JK - Great moment!

TD - Was this just one more movie you were asked to make a trailer for?

JK - As this was "The Rocky Horror Picture Show", ," it was a unique and quite distinctive experience for me as a young (ish) person and trailer maker.

TD - Did you experience the stage play as part of your approach to making the trailer?

JK - We (myself and some of the studio marketing people) all saw "The "Rocky Horror Show," as a theatrical production before the movie was shot. I don't think any of us was prepared for it, or necessarily completely "got it", ," but the younger among us thought it was funny and "pretty cool", ," and the music was great. The more adult among us expressed less enthusiasm...more of a WTF???

95

Response. And I don't think anyone walked away with any real idea of how to "sell" it until later when Tim Deegan came up with the midnight show plan.

TD - Some time later, when you saw the first cut of the film, how did you react?

JK - I was based in New York, and the Fox marketing people (back then, they were called Ad-Pub) were now in LA. My reaction was very positive. I thought the movie was smart, bold, different, fun, and probably hard to represent really well in 2-3 minutes (trailers were longer then than they are now).

TD - Was there a general formula for making trailers that you used?

JK - Until around 1967, almost all movie trailers were very much alike...big claim copy "*Never Before....,*" "*In a time....,*" etc., then narration telling the story, interspersed with short dialogue or action scenes, then a cast montage (some giving each star a dialogue moment, some just ID Shots) and then some final claims, and out. None of that would apply to "The Rocky Horror Picture Show," which defied the storytelling convention, used songs as part of the narrative, and had a cast of complete unknowns.

TD - How did that general approach fit for "Rocky Horror"?

JK - Usually, when I started working on a trailer, the studio had some idea of how they wanted to sell it. However, I don't remember getting any specific "direction" about the "Rocky Horror" trailer from Fox. Jonas and Johnny were still pretty WTF? You had not yet emerged as the champion of taking the movie to midnight as the ultimate way of marketing "Rocky Horror."

TD - So, you were pretty much left on your own to come up with an approach?

JK - I knew that telling the story with conventional narration would not capture the crazy, iconoclastic essence of the film. I wanted to try to let the film speak for itself as much as possible. That technique had worked well for me on "The Graduate," "Midnight Cowboy," and "The Lion In Winter".

TD - But that's not what happened.

JK - When I was breaking down the movie into its "trailer useable" out-of-context moments, I sensed it wouldn't work as a story-chronological montage. I realized it needed a more "set-up/punctuation" structure that could jump around playfully. I think that's when I decided to use the lips that were already a part of the film's opening as a visual narrative tool.

TD - How did you do that?

JK - It meant I would have to fake the copy over the existing lips, which would probably suck, or shoot new lips which actually spoke the trailer copy on camera: *"You've seen all kinds of movies, but you've never seen anything like The Rocky Horror Picture Show"*...and so on. So that was my plan. And I happened to know an actress (Rhea Ruggiero), who had perfect lips and teeth and a great sexy voice. So far, so good.

TD - Was that easy to do?

JK - I wasn't sure how to isolate just the lips, speaking (therefore moving) over a black screen. This was 1975, and CGI was not a tool we had handy. There was rotoscoping (which was what they called the process of matte-ing a moving subject), but that was very expensive and usually looked crappy around the edges. I watched the feature opening many times and thought maybe they had used black makeup...or shot the mouth through a small hole in a sheet of black velvet. I tested both and it wasn't working. The makeup was too shiny, and the pinhole wasn't very precise. I'm not sure *why* I didn't contact the "Rocky Horror" filmmakers to ask how they did theirs. Maybe I didn't want to seem like an amateur. Anyway, to be perfectly honest, I think I just decided to get the dullest possible black face makeup...and go for it. Fortunately, it worked. And the rest is – you know.

TD - What do you feel about the fact that the trailer you created for "Rocky Horror" is the longest continuously running theatrical trailer in movie history?

JK - I am thrilled to hear that my "Rocky Horror" trailer had the kind of useful life you describe. Thanks to the midnight show phenomenon. I definitely had no idea that would happen.

Meet Rhea Ruggiero - the lips for the trailer (7)

And, who was the person behind what Jeff Kanew called those "perfect lips and teeth and a great sexy voice"? They belong to actor Rhea Ruggiero, who now calls herself, "The most famous Lips, Voice, and Mouth in the longest-running trailer in American Film". Or, as she says, Jeff refers to her as "The most successful spokes mouth in movie history".

TD - Was becoming the lips on the trailer for "The Rocky Horror Picture Show" the start of commercial making for you?

RR - I had already done "Godfather 2", and a few national network on-camera commercials with Bob Giraldi..(king of commercials). Commercials were becoming a big deal back then..... but, when I met Jeff Kanew, who would hire me to be in the "Rocky Horror" trailer as the voice and lips, it was at the beginning of my career.

TD - What was the commercial advertising scene like at the time?

RR - Being an actor in the 1970's was very different than it is now. The 70's was a time when an actor could walk into any agent, production company, or ad agency, give them a headshot and resume, get hired, and make good friends. There was no script on how to do this, which is why it was so fun! You could develop relationships with all the creatives you met.

It was theater, on-camera commercials, voice overs, and soaps. That was New York in the 70's. All the doors were pretty much open. Today, when you go to an audition, the security is so tight, it's more like walking into a prison, they have to scan your i. d. before you can even walk to the elevators.

TD - How did you connect with Jeff Kanew?

RR - I was making "the rounds" one day, when I walked into Utopia Productions on 55th Street, and gave my picture to Jeff Kanew. I introduced myself, and we talked. Soon after, I auditioned for a feature film radio spot, with his brother Gary, who ran Radio Vendors, a branch of Utopia that Jeff was running with Gary.' They hired me. I may have been the only woman doing radio spots for feature films at that time. It was such a male-dominated niche.

TD - Had you done any work for Jeff by then, or just with his brother?

RR - One day, while at their production house, Jeff said, "I have this interesting idea for a movie trailer; it's called, "The Rocky Horror Picture Show," and I think you'd be perfect for it." I had no idea of the movie or what it was about. He showed me the copy.. then said, "But you have to be in black face, and it's only your mouth, lips, and voice." I trusted Jeff, so I said yes.

TD - What was the shoot like?

RR - The day I went in to do the shoot, I was a little nervous, not knowing what to expect. They painted my face black all around towards my ears, the whole jaw area, and under my nose. There may have been a makeup artists there. They put tissue around my neck so my clothes wouldn't get dirty. I had my hair up, and as they were applying the makeup, I was thinking.. Oh, will I ever be able to get this black makeup off?

TD - How did Jeff create the lips so perfectly?

RR - They gave me the reddest, wettest lips, I've ever seen with this lipstick to wear. We shot this in the hallway of Utopia. I was leaning up against the wall, and the camera was right up to my face, ; I could hardly move. They had pinned the copy close to me, so I could see it while they were filming. Remember, this was film, not digital, so time was money...of course, that added to my being a bit nervous. This was very unusual, to say the least, but I knew it was something distinctive. As well, this may have been the very first time a woman, was ever hired to do a trailer that actually played in the movie theaters!

TD - Did it come easy to you?

RR - Once we did one take, I was fine. I took a deep breath, focused, gave it my all...and said those famous first lines: "You've seen all kinds of movies, but you've never seen anything like 'The Rocky Horror Picture Show'.

TD - Did you know anything about either the play or movie version of "Rocky Horror"?

RR - Since I had never seen the film before the making of the trailer, I had no idea how lucky I was to be a part of 'The Rocky Horror Picture Show'. And how resilient, provocative and instrumental the trailer was, and still is, contributing to its success and phenomenon.

TD - How do you feel about your lips being a part of pop culture?

RR - Now, I may have the most famous lips in Hollywood! The trailer has played continuously for fifty years! Everyone wants to be acknowledged for their talent and accomplishments. So, I'm thrilled to be known for this. I love that it's so creative and original: . I say: Don't Just Dream It, Live it!

Notes:

1. http://tobacco.stanford.edu/tobacco_web/images/brpdf/marlboro/marlboro_history.pdf)

2. https://www.independent.co.uk/life-style/fashion/red-lips-hold-mens-gaze-longer-than-nude-ones-2150543.html).

3. https://www.youtube.com/watch?v=0j72Ckq0d-8

4. to author 7/29/19

5. to author 10/30/20

6. to author 7/17/19

7. to author 3/10/2020

Chapter 10
The LGBTQ+ Friendly Lou Adler

*A producer
stakes his movie's success on what was then a fringe audience.*

When Playboy Magazine was launched in 1953, Lou Adler was 20 years old and perfectly situated in the lower end of a desirable male demographic range to be attracted, like others in his generation, to the fantasy world of the sexualized objectification of women created by publisher Hugh Hefner.

Whether he looked at the magazine's famous photography or not, Lou could not have missed the cultural impact of such a groundbreaking and open display of sexuality. He has often been exactly tuned into the prevailing zeitgeist of the day. That sensitivity may account for his timely urge to contour an identity connected with beautiful and desirable women, an archetype promoted by Hefner.

Lou actualized that with a marriage to twenty-year-old television heartthrob Shelley Fabares in 1964 when he was thirty-one, and then a relationship with Swedish screen beauty and "Bond girl" Britt Ekland, who mothered their son Nicholai and would become the very special godmother of "Rocky Horror".

He carefully curated his mystique and image that was further contextualized and externally expressed by driving a pastel Ferrari Daytona Spider convertible and a white Rolls Royce, and living in a pink Bel Air mansion on Stone Canyon Road and at a formidable bespoke stone Malibu beach house as social signals of "arrival" status flexed by what had been a boy raised in poverty. It was a familiar rags-to-riches Horatio Alger-in-Hollywood trope.

He would later say that he "never was interested in getting big in Hollywood...other than dating actresses". (1) He has been publicly connected with several of them including Fabares, Ekland, and sisters Daryl and Page Hannah. Others like Julie Christie and Michelle Philips, have been linked to him.

Over the years, Lou fathered five sons with two actresses: Nicholai whose mom is Britt Ekland, and Manny, Ike, Oscar and Pablo, who call Page Hannah Adler mom. Son Cisco's mom is a civilian. He also has a son and daughter, Sonny and Honey, whose mom is the Danish model Winnie Hollman.

His association with Hollywood glamour, the cars and the houses, could be a type of visibly "living well as the best revenge" for a poverty-stricken childhood which was a statement he once bannered across the facade of The Roxy, a Sunset Strip club he owned, as he continued to design his public face.

Ever nimble, and always tuned into the pulse of the day, by the time he was forty, the fulcrum tipped and Adler expanded his worldview to embrace what was then known as "homosexuals" by taking a huge creative risk connecting with "The Rocky Horror Show", a London stage production created by Richard O'Brien, in which the very gay Dr. Frank 'N Furter tells an unsuspecting Brad Majors that "In just seven days I can make you a man". He staged it at the Roxy and then, with Michael White who staged the play in London, executive produced the movie version of the play.

The hyper-hetero young Hollywood playboy's embrace of the gay community, when he was already a celebrity rock and roll millionaire and didn't have to take this risk, was counter to the prevailing 1970's cultural wars against anything gay. It may have been another of his knacks for knowing what was culturally relevant,

Either for opportunity or for empathy, Lou stepped out of a personal comfort zone and into the emerging gay counterculture in what could retrospectively be viewed as a consciously courageous decision. If it was just a commercial opportunity bet, it paid off handsomely once the movie went into a midnight run in theaters across the country.

Although the movie's audience has diversified over the decades, in the foundational years his bet paid off: the gay audience substantially enriched Adler and distributor 20th Century Fox among others. As Fan Club Founder and President Sal Piro said "The gay community was there from the beginning". (2) They got it going; Lou's decades-long commercial connection with the gay community had begun.

It's an anomaly that Adler, playing against type, presented such a heterosexual ideal in his public and social life, but would make a sizable fortune in his business life from a movie that had, and still has, such a huge LGBTQ+ fan base.

He continued to capture the moment as recently as 2016 when he (as producer) and director Kenny Ortega cast Laverne Cox, an African-American transgender person, in "The Rocky Horror Picture Show: Let's Do the Time Warp Again" that was broadcast on the Fox Television Network on October 20.

His association with the gay community and his important role in the emergence of queer cinema add to Adler's legacy.

This is why what Lou did was culturally so important. In his Huff Post essay, "Why 'The Rocky Horror Picture Show' Remains A Queer Cinematic Milestone", Curtis M. Wong, the HP Senior Reporter (formerly Senior Editor, Queer Voices) says "Much of its 'midnight movie' success can be attributed to LGBTQ+ audiences, who identified with its embrace of sexual freedom, its objectification of men for a gay gaze and, of course, its unforgettable song-and-dance sequences." (3) Wong credits cultural critic Matt Baume with stating the proposition that 'Rocky Horror' is a movie by, for and about people who feel like aliens and outsiders. And the movie says to them, 'Don't worry, you're not alone — people like us can find each other at parties in the movie, and parties in real life.' He believes the film's inclusive message that life is best for those who, to paraphrase a famous line, give themselves over to absolute pleasure would have had an even deeper resonance among LGBTQ+ people who came of age in the early years after Stonewall". (4)

Movie producer Lou Adler was saying exactly the same thing years before "Queer Cinema" was formally identified by Ruby Rich as a genre of filmmaking in a groundbreaking essay in "Sight and Sound", the prestigious British film magazine published by the British Film Institute.

Associated with many other pop culture and societal trends Lou Adler, fifteen years before the term "queer cinema" was coined to describe movies like "Rocky Horror", may retroactively be seen as having been at the forefront of the genre, breaking new ground, again—this time for queers—as he had for years as a pop culture avatar in his very successful music producer career.

Adler embraced a then-fringe audience that would not only find community and inclusion at the midnight shows, but one that would help generate tens of millions of dollars of profits for a half-century of non-stop "Rocky Horror" theatrical play, home video and DVD sales, record sales, and miscellaneous merchandising.

"The gay community was there from the beginning," said "Rocky Horror" Fan Club founder Sal Piro. (5) They got it going. If producers Lou Adler and Michael White were bakers, the queer community could be like the yeast used to raise their dough. To continue the metaphor, Richard O'Brien, who wrote the book, music and lyrics of the original stage production and co-wrote the screenplay with Jim Sherman, could be seen as the secret ingredient that satisfied the tastes of so many moviegoers.

The historic, transgressive success and social impact of "The Rocky Horror Picture Show", and its theme of "Don't Dream It, Be It" has connected tens of thousands of LGBTQ+ and other moviegoers over three generations. The movie is a leading example of one of the most inclusive forms of cinema—what the academic B. Ruby Rich, in 1992, coined as "queer cinema", also known popularly as "LGBTQ+ cinema". Rich used the term "to define and describe a movement in queer-themed independent filmmaking in the early 1990s as an inclusive way of describing gay, lesbian, bisexual and transgender identity and experience, and also defining a form of sexuality that was fluid and subversive of traditional understandings of sexuality"

"Rich's perspective was that films of the New Queer Cinema movement typically share certain themes, such as the rejection of heteronormativity and the lives of LGBTQ+ protagonists living on the fringe of society." (6) While the Hollywood movie "Kiss of the Spider Woman" (1985) is often used as an early example of "queer cinema", the fact is that a decade earlier "The Rocky Horror Picture Show" (1975) was reaching a LGBTQ+ audience years before the Rainbow Flag and Pride festivals, and the inclusive unity they represent, were introduced.

As Adler has said about the "Rocky Horror" audience: "They may have been outcasts in the sense that they didn't have the same joys or seek the same outlets — sports, or music, or romance or whatever — as other people. They found their outlet in 'The Rocky Horror Picture Show'. I think the "Rocky Horror" fans are the happiest people in the world. Every Friday and Saturday night they have someplace to go where they can be with 300 people they like, and have a good time". (7)

"The Rocky Horror Picture Show" was both ahead of its time and, a half-century later, is timeless.

Was "The Rocky Horror Picture Show" part of the 1970's culture wars, and was Lou Adler implicit in the placement of it onto what became a gay agenda for public expression and support years before the Rainbow Flag and Pride festivals were introduced?

Was he ahead of his time about what he was doing, when none of his contemporaries showed that kind of public awareness and acknowledgment of the LGBTQ+ community? He had already established himself as one of the leading record producers in Southern California, even earning a referential accolade as a father of "sunshine pop" music. Did he really understand he was on track, with "Rocky Horror", to become a LGBTQ+ daddy.

His launch of "The Rocky Horror Show", the stage version that played at his Roxy nightclub on the Sunset Strip and at Broadway's Belasco theater, and then followed by the movie version of the play ("The Rocky Horror Picture Show") could not be mistaken for what it was at a bare minimum: a gay-friendly entertainment at a time of hostility against gays; when being a member of the almost-secret Mattachine Society was one of the few group options to express gay identity.

The cultural environment for gays, as Lou was preparing "Rocky Horror" was either camp or agitprop: riots and protests at gay bars (like the Stonewall and Black Cat incidents), or divas at the piano bar. After all, Bette Midler had already caused an underground sensation by performing in New York's gay Continental Baths in 1970, in an outrageous act supported by her pianist and songwriter

Barry Manilow. Camp and a celebration of gay togetherness was fine in the early 70's, as long as it was not too public.

Adler, by bringing "The Rocky Horror Show" to his stage at The Roxy brought a gay-friendly, campy story about "a sweet transvestite from transexual Transylvania" to a hip Sunset Strip audience at a time in the 1970's when the Strip was the epicenter of Southern California cool, and a home to a more traditional rock and roll culture. The club, which would quickly become a place where discoveries were made, opened on October 23, 1973; "The Rocky Horror Show" began its run less than six months later on March 24, 1974.

Lou's nightclub booking of "The Rocky Horror Show" as one of his earliest acts was sure to attract attention and give The Roxy a high-profile programming launch. It eventually led to a movie version of the play. At the same time, and for many years afterward, a music hangout near The Roxy called Barney's Beanery proudly advertised the side they took in the culture wars by hanging a sign that said "Faggots Stay Out". Lou had already picked his side.

Often considered as being ahead of the cultural curve, Los Angeles audiences welcomed "The Rocky Horror Show" by supporting a nine-month-long run at The Roxy. At the same time, easterners mostly shunned the Broadway production at the Belasco Theater, which expired after 45 performances.

This binary—success in the West but not the East, may have accurately reflected cultural attitudes that were as polarized as the distance between the Pacific and Atlantic coasts. Open-minded versus shut-out, in the early 70's culture wars.

For him to think that he could extend the brand by making a movie version of "The Rocky Horror Show", and play it successfully across the country adds to the impression that Adler was secure within himself and comfortable taking a big, national cultural risk of backing the queer community at a time of cultural war: that moviegoers would embrace his new and edgy entertainment featuring men in fishnets; a risk he did not need to take.

His Carole King records (mainly "Tapestry") were topping the charts, so he didn't really need success with a movie or to even make one at all. He could rely on King's golden ballads and the very popular Mommas and the Papas and their California dreaming vibe. And, he had the popular stoner comics Cheech and Chong in the wings. He did not have to attach his name and reputation to "Rocky Horror" and take a big leap away from the romanticism that had identified his "sunny sound" going back to the early surf tunes of Jan and Dean whom he managed, and make a transition from sunshine to darkness in his choice of material, or to step out of music and into movies.

Events in what would be credited to the "gay liberation" movement bracketed Adler's early identification with "The Rocky Horror Show" and "The Rocky Horror Picture Show." On one side was the "Black Cat Protest" on February 11, 1967, in the Silver Lake neighborhood of Los Angeles, where the community protested a police raid on the gay-friendly Black Cat tavern in a public show of outrage. Two years later, the violent "Stonewall riots" on June 28, 1969, at a gay bar in Greenwich Village, caught national attention and became a seminal event in the gay rights movement.

On the other side of "Rocky Horror's" 1974 intro, Florida oranges were on the agenda. Anita Bryant, a TV personality and Florida Orange Juice spokesperson, in 1977 led a very divisive and public campaign against the Dade County (home of Miami Beach) ordinance that prohibited discrimination on the basis of sexual orientation. Her aim, along with her Christian supporters, was to repeal the ordinance. Facing her was a national boycott of Florida orange juice, led by gay rights activists, who won the day and made Bryant a pariah, effectively ending her campaign.

Through most of this, Hollywood conducted business as usual, and celebrity support for gays and their issues was muted. It was in this cultural environment that Lou Adler went into production with a work that he used to challenge possibly scared and isolated young people: "Don't dream it, be it"...some paternal advice to disenfranchised kids.

He was ahead of the curve in the culture wars of the 70s by making "Rocky Horror" at a time when what society today takes for granted as LGBTQ+ was not even on the horizon. The Rainbow Flag was still years away. In a metaphorical sense, maybe the only "flag" those kids had to rally around was "Rocky Horror", as a safe refuge for a couple of hours on weekend nights.

Lou has maintained his outreach to the LGBTQ+ friendly community by continually supporting the "Rocky Horror" Fan Club and celebrating the community every half-decade with "Rocky Horror" anniversary parties and fan conventions that acknowledge not only the longevity of the movie but the fans themselves. "Hedwig and the Angry Inch", a play (and movie) that celebrates "gender-identity", was staged twice at Adler's Roxy in 2006 and 2012. More recently, Lou combined with Kenny Ortega in making "The Rocky Horror Picture Show: Let's Do the Time Warp Again" (2016), featuring an ethnic, transgender female in the role that Tim Curry made famous.

Today's LGBTQ+ world is fully fleshed out, not the skeleton in the closet that it was when Lou Adler made his decision to acquire the rights to stage and then film a story about "sweet transvestites...". None of his contemporaries can match that, nor do they have the accomplishment in the LGBTQ+ community that suggests how courageous Lou Adler was; so far ahead of the times.

Notes:

1. to author 12/17/19

2. interview with author 5/20/19

3. Huff Post 10-17-18 https://www.huffpost.com/entry/rocky-horror-picture-show-musical-matt-baume_n_5bc63c51e4b0a8f17ee6be26

4. ibid

5. interview with author 5/20/19

6. "New Queer Cinema" by Ruby Rich, Sight & Sound Magazine, September 1992

7. Page 35 "The Rocky Horror Picture Show Book" by Bill Henkin - Hawthorn Press, New York (1979)

Chapter 11
Under The Shadow of "Star Wars"…A Case Study

Looming over everything at Fox was an unknown movie that would explode the movie business.

The first time I saw "Rocky Horror" it was from a front-row seat at The Roxy, where the stage play was selling out. My first encounter with "Star Wars" was watching it from a couch in George Lucas' living room in his Marin County home.

"The Rocky Horror Picture Show" and "Star Wars" were the yin and the yang of Fox releases in 1975 and 1977. There were so many parallels yet in such asymmetrical ways.

I was the Fox advertising manager for "Rocky Horror" and the Fox director of advertising for "Star Wars". They have never been presented side-by-side in a case study like this that, for each movie, examines the:

- Acquisition of rights

- Production

- First look

- Release strategy

- Sneak previews

- Creative advertising

- Marketing plan

- Merchandising

- Fan base

"Star Wars", as the world soon knew, became one of the biggest blockbuster movies and generational touchstones in history. But, "The Rocky Horror Picture Show" was as big a cultural phenomenon, and arguably as profitable on a "return on investment" basis, the ROI metric that companies use to measure net profitability. And both have been in continuous release one way or another, the multiple spin-offs of "Star Wars" and the continuously running--for fifty years--of the "Rocky Horror" midnight shows.

Before exploring how these two movies were handled, it's important to contextualize Twentieth Century-Fox Film Corporation at that time: it was topsy-turvy. The studio announcement, in late winter 1974, was terse and tumultuous. There had been a management shakeup--Fox President Gordon Stulberg, who had given the green light to producer Lou Adler for Fox to acquire the distribution rights to "The Rocky Horror Picture Show" from him and Michael White was out.

Adler suddenly had no executive to run high-level interference for the movie if needed. Bob Sherman, the production vice president who played an important role in acquiring the movie for Fox, had left the studio to produce a Marlon Brando movie, "Missouri Breaks" (1976), at United Artists.

I had not yet met Adler and would not until a fateful studio meeting where I told him I didn't like his movie. But, can you be objective about marketing it, he asked. Yes, I told him I was a professional, and my personal feelings would not get in the way. From that moment in 1975, I became his single point of contact at the studio.

Relationships make a big difference in Hollywood, and Lou had lost his man-at-the-top access at Fox, so I was going to have to fill a big void. I knew who Adler was as a record producer and listened to his music. I guessed (correctly) that he would not be the typical producer I knew at the studio. He came from a different world, that of music. And had practically no movie-making experience, so everything was fresh with no preconceived ideas of how things should be done.

Everyone at the studio wondered when and where the fallout of Stulberg's sudden departure would hit next. As reported by the Los Angeles Times, "Stulberg left abruptly at the end of 1974, citing "policy differences with the company"--in reality, differences with Stanfill". (1) The executive building hallways were full of rumors, but board chairman Stanfill quickly settled down the speculation by creating a management "troika" of three Fox executives who became executive vice presidents of Fox, reporting to Stanfill. It consisted of Alan Ladd, Jr. as production head, David Raphael as worldwide distribution head, and William Immerman as head of business and legal affairs.

Production of "The Rocky Horror Picture Show" was from October 21 to December 19, 1974, so Lou would have just been wrapping up principal photography when the Stulberg news broke.

I asked Lou if he had a reaction to the loss of his point person at Fox, if there was a hand-off, or if he just continued on independently and eventually delivered a print to Fox and had his meeting with the marketing and distribution team? "I just continued" Lou told me, in an example of how different it was to work as an independent producer outside the politics of the studio system. (2)

Not long after the departure of Stulberg, Laddie emerged as Fox President and became the single most important Fox executive for "Rocky Horror" at the time by telling me to "go ahead and try it" when I asked him to let me take "Rocky Horror" into the midnight market, something that was vigorously opposed by almost everyone else on the Fox marketing and distribution team.

As George Lucas pointed out for "Star Wars" about his relationship with Alan Ladd, Jr. as President of Fox, Ladd "Invested in me, he did not invest in the movie" (3)

I felt the same about my interaction with the studio boss. I pitched him with passion, not content. When I met with Laddie to pitch the midnight show concept, I knew he had never seen the movie or met with Adler. He had inherited "Rocky Horror". First, he asked me to explain what a midnight show was, and then to tell him how much money I thought it would make at midnight. I took a wild guess because no studio had ever released a movie at midnight and confidently projected a box office gross of $5 million. That was a pretty aggressive assertion, for in those days that was a lot of money. The shooting budget for "Star Wars" was also $5 million (although it would rise dramatically). In hindsight, I could see that Laddie was investing in me just like he invested in Lucas. Not the product but the person and their passion for the product.

All I needed was Laddie's backing, and, at that point, it was just Laddie who believed in me and me who believed in "The Rocky Horror Picture Show". He had a studio to run (and his big gamble "Star Wars") so, ultimately, it was just me and my persistence and perseverance if "Rocky Horror" was to have any success.

It was not just Stulberg's leaving that was causing a shadow. George Lucas had begun principal photography on "Star Wars" in March 1976, a few months after Stulberg left. Like an eclipse of the sun, this movie was casting a long shadow across Fox. It was one of two movies Fox did not know what to do with because, for "Star Wars", all Lucas would say was its cowboys and indians in outer space. Laddie was clearly betting on George. The other was "The

Rocky Horror Picture Show", a movie that defied categorization other than it was something about sweet transvestites from transexual Transylvania. Both wound up being blockbuster surprises for Fox.

Everything happening with "The Rocky Horror Picture Show" was happening under the long and deep shadow of "Star Wars". Everyone knew what a huge risk making that movie was...the budget had ballooned from five to eight million, and then eleven million dollars, that almost cost Ladd his job and created panic inside the studio walls.

Lou Adler's $1,300,000 budget for "Rocky Horror" was an under the radar piece of cake, by comparison. Unlike "Star Wars", which had so many high-level eyes on it, starting with board chairman Dennis Stanfill uneasy with the escalating production costs, "The Rocky Horror Picture Show" was never mentioned in the executive suite.

Filmmaker George Lucas had an aversion to coming to Hollywood from his Marin County home in Northern California, so he was not available, like other filmmakers, to help manage expectations about his work. Like Lucas, Lou did not like studio meetings and attended only the one where I met him, and then shifted to one-on-one offsite meetings at his Sunset Strip nightclub, The Roxy, his Ode Records office at A&M Records, his Bel Air mansion or his Malibu beach house office with me instead of coming into the Fox studio.

Everyone at Fox was working hard to get "The Other Side of Midnight" ready to be the big summer picture from Fox in 1977. It was to be released on June 8, 1977, two weeks after the May 25, 1977 opening of "Star Wars" that, in the early stages before it was screened by Fox executives, was planned to be sent into the market as a limited release sci-fi genre movie.

"The Other Side of Midnight" was based on a best-selling novel by Sidney Sheldon that had been ranked at number one on The New York Times Best Seller list. Sheldon's formula novels that were targeted to women, as the movie would be, full of suspense and drama. Producing this major movie that was Fox's hope for a big summer at the box office was Frank Yablans, a former head of Paramount and a future head of MGM/UA. In between stints as a studio mogul with a reputation as being a tough "heavy", Yablans was sitting in his third-floor suite of the Fox Executive Building, calling the shots on how the studio would handle his movie. It was rare to have a former studio head in that position, and his successful "Silver Steak" (1976) for Fox helped get him known by the ranks as a demanding producer.

Little did Yablans, or anyone, expect that "Star Wars" would push "The Other Side of Midnight" aside into darkness and not be the big summer hit for Fox in 1977.

Larry Gleason recounted that, "I was president of Mann Theaters, which had the Chinese in Hollywood and theaters in Westwood. There were a lot of people at Fox who didn't want to make "Star Wars". The running joke was that when George Lucas made his final pitch to Alan Ladd Jr., who was running Fox at the time, Laddie said no, but he said it so softly that nobody heard him. In those days, you had studio customers. Mann's main customers were Paramount and Warner Bros. Once in a while, you'd play a picture from someone else.

Fox's general sales manager at the time, the late Peter Myers, called and said George Lucas really wanted the Chinese. We had two weeks available before we had to play William Friedkin's

"Sorcerer" from Paramount. Fox has such limited expectations for the film he said that two weeks would be all they needed.

After opening weekend, we went to Paramount, but they wouldn't budge. They said we had to live up to our commitment, but we wanted to keep control of "Star Wars". We owned another theater in Hollywood that wasn't very nice. It stayed open 24 hours, so people slept there. We did a crash renovation, put in new seats, painted it, and cleaned it up. We moved "Star Wars" there, was played for two weeks before coming back to the Chinese. (4)

The one-two punch of "Star Wars" and the midnight shows of "The Rocky Horror Picture Show" would launch Fox into the future: midnight shows had never been tried by a studio before, and special effects like in "Star Wars" had never been seen before. Yablan's and Sheldon's movie was suddenly an outdated box-office disappointment.

The two movies followed the pattern of how movies get made and sold, starting with the acquisition of the rights.

Re Acquisition

Acquiring "Rocky Horror" by Fox must have appeared magical to producer Lou Adler. All it took, he thought, was an affirmative nod of her head by Helen Stulberg, wife of the studio head, after she saw the stage play at the Roxy to clinch the deal.

In reality, her husband Gordon was equivocal; he would not agree to acquire the movie until, unbeknownst to Adler and the others, he had a secret silent partner to help pay for the cost. That investor, John Heyman, later said it was the most successful movie investment he ever made.

What Fox was acquiring was the negative pick-up rights to the movie, meaning for a certain amount of cash producers produce the movie off the lot and away from the studio with no studio oversight. The finished movies were then distributed by the studio. It was categorized as an independent movie, not a studio movie.

George Lucas used the traditional route of having Tom Pollack, a powerhouse Hollywood attorney, negotiate with Fox in conjunction with Lucas's agent, Jeff Berg.

The story was told in an interview with Mike Fleming Jr. in the publication Deadline on October 18, 2015, (5)

"Jeff Berg, who was George's agent, took the treatment to Alan Ladd Jr at Fox and Laddie said yes, I'll make this, and they negotiated the outline of the deal. George got $50,000 to write, another $50,000 to produce, and $50,000 to direct." That was the starting point, but several iterations of the deal followed involved merchandising rights and a sequel. The initial production budget was five million dollars which ballooned to eight million and caused a panic in the studio and with the board of directors when it hit eleven million dollars.

Production

Producers Lou Adler and Michael White and director Jim Sharman had no need to rehearse their "Rocky Horror" cast when it arrived on location at the Bray Studio near Maidenhead in Berkshire, England. The same cast from the stage play that ran for nine months at the Roxy would repeat their roles in the movie version.

Because it was not a movie produced by Fox, the producers had no studio involvement, although some of Fox's European marketing team visited the set for the filming of the climactic swimming pool scene. "There was dead silence; "They didn't stay for lunch" Lou Adler later told the New York Times. (6)

The "Star Wars" filming took place on sound stages in England and some exterior locations. Other than budget increases Laddie fought for with Fox chairman Dennis Stanfill, there was very little known about "Star Wars" as it was filming.

First Looks and Release Strategies

As soon as practical after filming was completed, both movies were made available to Fox executives to start developing release strategies.

Lou Adler could not have met a colder reception for "The Rocky Horror Picture Show" when he screened it at Fox. I was present in what had been Daryl F. Zanuck's private screening room in the basement of the Fox Executive Building, with its hidden stairway to his office (now occupied by Laddie), when Lou showed a group of us marketing and distribution executives a rough cut of his movie."When it ended...nobody said a word...then they quickly walked out..." (7)

Nobody knew what to do with this movie. Playing it ultra-safe, the studio did a direct copy of the advertising that had been used for the stage show. It accomplished two things. One was to quickly give a marketing department that wanted nothing to do with the movie a fast and inexpensive way to develop a campaign. It also allowed them to tell the producer they felt like sticking with a proven advertising winner was the best approach. What worked for the Roxy stage presentation in LA, they hedged, would be just as good in attracting a regular-run theatrical audience in Los Angeles.

Lou Adler was really at the mercy of the studio on this, without any leverage, his powerlessness accentuated by the fact he was from the music business not the movie business. The two executives he had a working relationship with were studio president Gordon

Stulberg and production vice president Robert Sherman, had both left Fox. Lou was friendless at Fox, and the movie was an orphan.

I was a very young 20-something and, although I had connected strongly with Lou, was not an upper level executive. However, I believed in myself and had ambition. At age 22, I had been by far the youngest executive at MGM where I was the MGM International Publicity Manager with a global remit while my contemporaries were still in college. I had my first job in the movie business, interning for Stanley Kubrick on "2001: A Space Odyssey", when I was 17. It did not help that most of my Fox bosses were three or four decades older than me. They seemed stuck in the past while I couldn't wait for tomorrow to arrive.

While I was in constant contact with Lou, I was always messaging him, and from him back to the studio, updated on the marketing and sales plan. I was more of a conduit than a decision-maker, but that would change as soon as the movie failed and was pulled from release and I began advocating for a midnight show.

Accessing "Star Wars" to begin thinking about a release strategy was a little trickier. Once filming was completed, studio president Alan Ladd, Jr., sent a small team of us executives from marketing and sales to see a workprint. Lucas preferred working from Northern California. The only time I, and my marketing and sales colleagues, ever saw him in person or spoke to Lucas in Los Angeles was at a party in Laddie's Beverly Hills home after the movie opened to huge box office. Laddie wanted George to meet the marketing and sales executives who were behind the very successful launch of "Star Wars".

The first work print screening for Fox was held at George's Marin County home close to San Francisco, in his living room, our small group sinking comfortably into plush couches and armchairs.

We had flown up after lunch, screened the movie, and returned to the studio in the late afternoon.

None of us were particularly overwhelmed, and told Laddie about our hesitation. He reminded us that all those crazy crayon markings in the black and white slop print were indications of where special effects would be inserted into the movie. Also missing was music, except for a piano "guide track" to indicate where music cues would be dropped into the movie. John Williams was already at work composing his spectacular score for the movie that would be added later. Laddie reminded everyone that George was using a new computer-driven technology for special effects, which would lead to the creation of Industrial Light and Magic, his special effects lab for the new technology. Using very sophisticated special effects to help carry a movie was groundbreaking.

Of course, when we did see the finished movie it wiped out any doubts. I, and everyone else from Fox in the Cary Grant Theater on the MGM studio lot was overwhelmed by the movie and knew instantly that we had a monster hit on our hands. The movie received a standing ovation and cheers from the executives and special guests seeing "Star Wars" for the very first time.

When the post-production supervisor was told to book a screening for the executives, the Daryl F. Zanuck Theater at Fox (its showcase theater of several on the lot) had already been booked, so he made arrangements with MGM, straight down Motor Avenue from Fox, for the screening. Suddenly, 'Star Wars" was the most important movie awaiting release.

The marketing campaign started to come alive, beginning with a poster that featured Hans Solo (Mark Hamill), Princess Leia (Carrie Fisher) and the outline of Darth Vader's helmet in the background. The slogan was "In a galaxy far, far away".

Sneak Previews

Studios like to get a feel for audience reaction to a movie by holding an out-of-town sneak preview. Both "Star Wars" and "The Rocky Horror Picture Show" had their sneaks, with polar opposite results.

For "Rocky Horror", we went to Santa Barbara, a seaside enclave about ninety miles north of Los Angeles. It was a cold opening for the audience—just a notice that a "sneak preview" would be held along with the regular feature. Not many in the audience even got to see Tim Curry make his entrance descending in the lift and belting out, "I'm just a sweet transvestite, from transexual Transylvania". That electrifying scene played to a mostly empty house. Most of the audience had already streamed out of the theater. "Tim Deegan was with the project from the beginning," said Adler. "He sat on the curb with me outside the theater in Santa Barbara. The only glimmer of hope was that there were four or five people who sat through it and came up after the film and thanked us for making that kind of film. We were really happy. It was almost like we made it for someone". (8)

About three weeks before the opening of "Star Wars", a sneak preview was held in San Francisco, and Cheryl Boone Isaacs (sister of Fox's "Star Wars" distribution majordomo Ashley Boone) recalled the crowd's reaction: "By the time that Millennium Falcon got across the screen, everybody was standing and screaming. I remember the guys — Laddie, Ashley, and all of them — were kind of huddled together and hugging." (9)

Research

There was no research program for "Rocky Horror". In another example of being polarly opposite to how "Star Wars" was being handled, Fox had a fully executed program that included focus groups and title and advertising testing. This full-blown research program was presented to David Weitzner, the newly hired VP of Advertising at Fox (and my new boss after Panama left for work at an advertising agency), and I was promoted to his job as Advertising Director; he recalled what he was up against.

"On my first day on the job at the studio," said Weitzner, "Alan Freeman, head of motion picture research at Fox, asked to see me. I had already met and worked with Alan at Palomar Pictures through Ed Sherick, a TV and movie producer whose movies "Sleuth" and "The Heartbreak Kid" I had worked on."

"Alan told me that "Star Wars" was going to bomb. His research showed it was a bad title. His focus groups said the title referred to science fiction, which did not appeal to women, and "wars," a word that women did not like.

Neither of his findings sat well with me or Laddie. In fact, women became an important part of the audience, thanks to their love for the character of Princess Leia (Carrie Fisher)."

"I was working as Vice President, General Manager at Grey Advertising, one of Madison Avenue's legendary agencies," said Weitzner, "before I accepted the job of VP Advertising that the new Fox studio head Alan Ladd, Jr. had offered me. There was a lag of four to five months between me being hired and moving to California. I would get calls from Laddie, at least weekly, and often more frequently, about "Star Wars"…he really believed in it. I never heard a word about "The Rocky Horror Picture Show", which had just started its midnight run. It was always "Star Wars".

"With "Star Wars", Fox went from seat of pants marketing to Madison Avenue marketing. We were very proud of what we had done because it brought methodology to how we spent money that no other studio was doing. Even the "Star Wars" campaign was difficult. George Lucas always had the image of what he wanted to do with "Star Wars" marketing. Part of the challenge was to invest in what Lucas wanted to do."

"There is a parallel with the two movies: "The Rocky Horror Picture Show" needed to be discovered. In point of fact, so did "Star Wars".

"From a marketing point of view, I saw a very interesting parallel between "The Rocky Horror Picture Show" and "Star Wars. Both films required a fan base to embrace and discover and like each movie. With "Star Wars", we were talking to them about what it was about. With "The Rocky Horror Picture Show", it was experiential. Both films needed to be discovered."

"This was in the era before Comic-Con, which has turned into a huge convention that caters to "fandom" and can generate tremendous awareness for a movie. "Fox hired Charlie Lippencott, a publicist who traveled all over the country to comic book conventions trying to pre-sell "Star Wars". Because of this, there was somewhat of a base audience that knew about "Star Wars" and showed up on opening day.

The opening of "Star Wars" was supported by a significant television campaign. We had lots of TV ads being bought. Doyle Dane Bernbach, a heavyweight Madison ad agency, was the studio's ad agency. We changed it up a little in how a studio dealt with its ad agency, and how the studio moved away from the status quo of not committing to the next week's ad budget until the Monday morning marketing meeting had reviewed the previous weekend's grosses. In general, each studio was making a week-by-week decision to continue or not continue supporting a film with television advertising.

"We created and published a marketing plan that went six weeks into the run of "Star Wars". It was the first time a plan went beyond pre-opening and first-week advertising support. My Madison Avenue background and training was to be ready to move immediately. There was a six-week flowchart to commit to "Star Wars" that we were asking for approval on so we could put money out there right away. This way, we could plan ahead and take advantage of certain efficiencies. Other studios didn't do it. One of the standouts of our media planning was that it took a longer point of view. That marketing plan was a professional approach to the release of "Star Wars".

"Merchandising was a little more dicey. There was almost no merchandising for "Star Wars", and not lots of merchandising activity at any studio. One film that had some merchandising was "Annie", but that was mainly t-shirts and posters, but no real push."

"Kenner Toys took a master license on the merchandising, but not until after the film opened and was a runaway hit. Sadly, no companies expressed interest in "Star Wars" merchandising prior to its spectacular opening. It was a slow process of six months for Kenner to render the characters and get them approved by George Lucas, and then have the toys and figures manufactured. We produced a stocking stuffer gift certificate, so that kids would be getting the toys, but it took months before the toys reached the marketplace. The stocking stuffer was instrumental and the only way we could offer merchandise because of the long lead time between Memorial Day, when the movie opened, and Christmas. Toys would not be available until early in the new year. Once the toys came out from Kenner, it exploded, supported by public demand and Fox marketing money as well as Kenner marketing money. Most merchandising came well after the film opened. It all came after the fact. Nobody wanted to touch "Star Wars" at the beginning." (10)

A year prior to the "Star Wars" opening and massive research and media plan that supported it, Fox opened "The Rocky Horror Picture Show" at the Waverly Theater with an advertising budget of $65. I had been allocated $75,000 to spend on advertising, but didn't touch it. Instead, I relied on my version of a marketing g plan that I called "discovery". The idea was to undersell the movie, just using the trailer on the Waverly screen and some small handouts to people going to the theater. It was the lips on a black background. With the "a different set of jaws" slogan. The Walter Reade Organization, owner of the Waverly, always ran a directory ad in the Village Voice showing what was playing at all their theaters and that was the only "newspaper" advertising for the movie. No radio, no promotion, just let it be discovered by moviegoers that may be caught by surprise by what they were being and therefore become amplified voices in a word of mouth campaign that would generate interest in the movie.

A few days before opening, I was called into the VP advertising and publicity's office and asked why I had not submitted my advertising plan to him for approval. He exploded when he learned I was not advertising the movie, just relying on my "discovery" strategy, but it was too late to do anything like run a full page in the New York Times, which was his idea. Thankfully, we were well past the deadline for that.

My minimalist "discovery" marketing plan has continued for five decades. There has never been an advertising deduction from box office receipts, meaning the profits fall directly and quickly to the bottom line where they are split with the theaters, the studio and profit participants.

While I was letting "Rocky Horror" sell itself, Fox was engaged in a massive marketing and media campaign that Weitzner and a Doyle Dane Bernbach account executive were creating and supervising.

The Media-Marketing Strategy for "Star Wars"

Neal Lemlein, the media executive charged with creating the media-marketing plan, shared the process with a deep dive into how it happened when he told me that "Our goal for "Star Wars" was to bring a more sophisticated and systematic approach to the communications planning in support of this unique film's theatrical introduction. I was fresh out of Madison Avenue advertising where I had been trained in media planning on the very demanding Procter and Gamble consumer packaged goods brands. Working with David Weitzner, the VP of Advertising at Fox, and with Susan Furedi, media supervisor at DDB, we developed a very innovative plan.

My initial observation of the media-marketing planning process in the film industry was that there was no process. A media plan usually just consisted of a list of TV shows in which commercials would air and a newspaper schedule. No strategy, no supporting analysis of the film's anticipated audience appeal, and little, if any, target audience demographic profiling.

We spent considerable time discussing appropriate positioning for "Star Wars" and concluded that it could be targeted to a broad base of moviegoers on many different levels. It had action adventure, intergalactic magic as a backdrop, a romantic story element, wonderfully drawn characters, and, in short, two hours of compelling entertainment for every moviegoing segment.

Our intention was to leave no stone unturned and to drive key levels of awareness and interest-in-seeing broadly for this extraordinary movie. We felt that a key strategy would be to drive overall, broad audience attention and interest, by attacking key market segments individually-sort of plans within an overall plan.

The campaign approach we took attempted to address multiple audience segments. The plan structure resembled a classic Madison Avenue, state-of-the-art marketing framework, and included stated objectives. We analyzed and defined the overall target audience definition and its subsets. We didn't realized it, but we were also revolutionizing the way film planning would be approached by the industry going forward.

This planning approach we took, known as segmentation strategy, really characterized the overall campaign direction. One effort was directed at young adults, another at parents, and another at kids. Still, another was aimed at parents with kids. A separate effort featured the film's romantic element. The challenge with using a segmentation strategy in film marketing is that you need to ensure that the various strategic directions taken do not create confusion and detract from the impact of the key overall message. Consistency is key. David Weitzner brilliantly created advertising that both delivered to the specific segments while also selling the overall unique and magical elements of this broad-based adventure.

I think the key audience trigger that we were able to pull with the media-marketing strategy had to do with what we call purchase influence. We recognized that "Star Wars" would deliver solidly to both kids and parents. By directing efforts to both segments separately and simultaneously, we created a push-pull dynamic whereby each segment influenced or nagged the other to attend. This worked extremely well.

Another strategy that characterized our approach was the phasing of the marketing effort. The entire campaign was structured into phases designed to first introduce and educate the audience and then to drive home the messaging. We did audience delivery analyses of each key moviegoing segment. Reach and frequency, the two pillars of media measurement, were used to objectify planned efforts for each key campaign phase; "teaser," pre-opening, and opening week. We also pre-planned contingency advertising support for post-opening advertising/media to be activated based on various opening weekend scenarios.

I think that this was the first time that the comprehensive communications flow chart we developed was used in film marketing. Our plan, with its intricate strategies, multiple targets, and phases, was challenging to explain and present. We decided to construct this one chart which detailed, on a timeline, all communications activity for each audience segment and campaign phase. This flow chart graphically displayed everything described in our 40-page media manual. It became the key exhibit for effectively presenting the entire campaign to studio heads and filmmakers. The chart was especially useful because, in addition to showing all communications plan activity by campaign day…it also depicted how all of the campaign's moving parts interacted for cumulative impact. This tool remains key in today's film marketing process.

I believe we also led the way in the area of media placement and negotiation. While in the late seventies, it would have been too early for the film category to be actively participating in what has become the upfront market for national broadcast –where advertising inventory and expenditures are committed to months in advance in order to gain increased purchasing efficiency and to insure program selectivity—we operated in a very similar fashion.

We analyzed programming options for specific viewer content and demographic fit with our strategic approach. We purchased our media as far in advance as possible and paid close attention to selectivity and efficiency. It was a very impactful media execution.

Looking back at the "Star Wars" campaign, I think the plan we developed was dynamic, extremely well thought out, and well ahead of its time. We built a crescendo of awareness and interest for the picture prior to its opening and word of mouth soon carried it to unprecedented greatness. In fact, in recalling one very noteworthy piece of post-opening research—three to four weeks after the film had opened, those on movie lines to see "Star Wars" around the country were interviewed. Amazingly, we learned that if a moviegoer had seen "Star Wars" even once, then the average number of times that moviegoer had seen it was 4+ times! Unbelievable.

I am grateful for having had the "Star Wars" planning experience. It was the first of many campaigns I participated in at several different studios. In transitioning from consumer goods media and advertising into film I soon realized how integral media marketing was to the entire film campaign process and how strategic solutions and approaches could have such an impact on the success of movies in the marketplace. (11)

Merchandise

"The Rocky Horror Picture Show" opened before the era of full-scale movie-related merchandising. Other than a soundtrack album from Lou Adler's Ode Records, whatever "merch" was available was created by fans on a cottage industry level. Over the years, the movie's "merch" has gotten more professional. In an undeniable mismatch, the merchandising rights are held by one of the greatest movie-related merchandising powerhouses in Hollywood--the Walt Disney Company that took the "merch" rights as part of their purchase of Twentieth Century Fox a few years ago.

The vast collection of "Star Wars" merchandise controlled by George Lucas, along with the movie profits, turned him into a billionaire. Like "Rocky Horror", "Star Wars" wound up at Disney.

Fans

There is no question that fans made "Rocky Horror" the success that it has become. Shortly after the opening of the midnight show at the Waverly Theater in Greenwich Village, the first theater to play the movie at midnight, I received a call at my Fox studio office from Sal Piro asking if there was a fan club and, if not, could he start one? After discussing with my Fox bosses and producer Lou Adler, I went back to Sal and said yes, but there would be no affiliation with Fox, no recognition, and no financial support. Lou Adler had suggested to me that it be fan-driven and, agreeing with him, that was the mandate that I gave to Sal.

Over the next few years, Sal worked tirelessly building the fan club. I would tell him what markets we were playing in, and he would find locals and invite them to join the fan club. Annual conventions, anniversaries, and other celebrations were a way of bringing the fans together in person. The cosplay aspect of the fan experience was a critical element. The fans were, and continue to be, relating to the movie's most heartfelt message "don't dream it be it".

The fan base for "Star Wars" was born at Comic-Con where the Fox-hired publicist Charlie Lippencott delivered the "Star Wars" message. The commercial licensing by Kenner Toys solidified the fan base.

Every movie has its own behind the scenes story. The fact that "The Rocky Horror Picture Show" and "Star Wars" were so closely related in time and space has provided a peek into two incredible journeys.

Notes:

1. (https://www.latimes.com/archives/la-xpm-2000-oct-18-me-38185-story.html

2. to author 12/31/2019

3. "Empire of Dreams: The Story of the Star Wars Trilogy" Star Wars Trilogy Box Set DVD documentary. [2004]

4. https://www.hollywoodreporter.com/heat-vision/star-wars-flashback-no-theater-wanted-show-movie-1977-846864

5. https://deadline.com/2015/12/star-wars-franchise-george-lucas-historic-rights-deal-tom-pollock-1201669419/

6. https://www.nytimes.com/2015/10/04/movies/rocky-horror-is-doing-the-time-warp-forever.html

7. to author 10/21/20

8. https://www.latimes.com/archives/la-xpm-1990-10-14-ca-3748-story.html

9. https://www.hollywoodreporter.com/features/he-was-star-wars-secret-weapon-why-was-he-forgotten-1275211

10. to author 1/15/21

11. to author 12/26/19

Chapter 12
"Oh God, My Dad's Wearing Fishnets and Heels..."

In Their Own Words - Wide-ranging recollections of personal "Rocky Horror" experiences.

Interviews with:

1. Becca Walsh
2. Mark Walsh
3. Lisa Sutton
4. Sal Piro
5. Larry Vizel
6. Tony Pazuzu
7. James Lajer and Joanna Stephens
8. MK Brown and Brett Mourglia
9. Kristian Fletcher
10. Amy Galaudet
11. Vito Russo
12. Lou Adler
13. Tim Deegan
14. Laddie
15. Mark Jabara
16. Matthew Jon Beck
17. Marc Mancini

18. Denis Stafill

19. Mike Shapiro

20. Tony Seiniger

21. Lorelei Shark

22. Jeff Kanew

23. Rhea Ruggiero

24. Jean Louis Rubin

25. David Weitzner

26. Tim Deegan

27. Neal Lemlein

28. Lani Jo Leigh

29. Seth Willenson

30. Bill Quigley

31. Tom Cooper

32. Barry Bostwick

Interviews:

1. Becca Walsh - "Oh God, my dad's wearing fishnets and heels..."

TD - What was your perception of your dad as a "Rocky Horror" fan / cast member when you were younger?

BW - I don't think my brother or I understood anything about "Rocky Horror" when we were young, or had any perception of what our Dad was doing as a "Rocky Horror" fan or cast member. It was the early '90s and the kids were not allowed to watch the home video, except up until the Time Warp, but no further.

One day, when I was 16, my parents were away and I watched the whole movie. OMG, my Dad was doing this! Seeing him doing Dr. Scott, being so different from how I usually saw him, was such an eye opening experience. Oh God, my dad's wearing fishnets and heels and gong around in a wheelchair. Suddenly, it was hey dad, lets go have fun. It was a bonding experience between us.

Some college age friends come over, we're doing "Rocky Horror". I knew some of the call backs.

TD - What got you into "Rocky Horror" as a fan? Are you a cast member?

BW - I'm not in the cast, but am an excited audience member. I yell very, very loudly. It's very fun for me. I don't go as often as my Dad, but certain nights I do—Halloween, Super Heroes, etc. I'll get in a costume and yell and scream.

In El Paso, in the early 90s my Mom was supportive up to you're not bringing it into the house. Nothing was said about Dad on Saturday nights when he was gone, or why he was gone. Once we moved to Austin, my Dad worked for the City. After Mom passed, Dad found his release in being stupid and silly, and being more active. Its done wonders for him. He was unapproachable but now, because of "Rocky Horror" he's my Dad, and he's my friend. It gave him a creative outlet.

TD - how long have you been part of the "Rocky Horror" experience?

BW - I've been participating in "The Rocky Horror Picture Show" on and off for about 10 years, and I've watched the growth of the experience. iIt's a double edge sword. There's a lot more audience appreciation, but also a lot more removal of audience appreciation. People go and have fun, with minimalist props. enjoying themselves, which is what the experience is all about.

"Rocky" Horror is a hard niche to enter..twice a month instead of weekly. That cut down on the craze of stepping outside your life for a minute. It's a leveler—everyone is enjoying the hell out of it. Come enjoy and let your boundaries be tested.

The professionalism of the shadow casts can be a little distancing. O'Brien Orchestra has gone from a low to a professional quality of people coming and it has gotten better. The quality of the technicalities has improved.

TD - Does watching the video offer a different experience than being in person at a midnight show?

BW - The video is the first way anyone that wants to participate should see "Rocky Horror", to be able to follow the plot. But, the stage version is about having fun. On the video, you can pause, and pay closer attention. That's what I did. If you are offended, you save the ticket price. It also provides an opportunity when a midnight show is not locally available, especially if kids that want to see it are too young to go out to the theater at midnight.

TD - Do you have any concerns now that Disney owns Fox and controls the fate of "The Rocky Horror Picture Show"?

BW - What if Disney were to say it's over, while Disney wants to portray an all American image.....it will not cost them anything to have this...the fans are driving it, there are no costs to Disney. Yes there would be an outcry, but most of the fans would say we'll have our own clandestine showing, doing things our own way. We'd do the Time Warp in the back yard. Why not?

TD - Any final thoughts?

BW - We have a much more open society. "Rocky Horror" is a creative way to express diversity without judgement or retribution.

2. Mark Walsh - "I've seen 'Rocky Horror' become multi-generational."

TD - What was your first impression of "The Rocky Horror Picture Show"?

MW - Seeing "Rocky Horror" for the first time was one of those things that just hit like a bomb. It was the perfect outlet for insanity. It was one of those understandings you just can't get it until you get there. For a certain slice of pop culture, it's a cultural item so embedded we can't get by without it. Just hearing the word "anticipation" can trigger you.

TD - Do you remember the first time you saw it?

MW - I was present the first night of "The Rocky Horror Picture Show" in San Antonio, Texas. As near as we've been able to establish, including at a San Antonio show earlier this year, I'm the "last man standing" for any SA RHPS cast from the 70s.

TD - What caused you to go see the movie in the first place?

MW - My roommate at Trinity University said we just have to go see this, so we went one Saturday night to the large multiplex at the intersection of the 410 and interstate highway 10, where "Rocky Horror" was playing. The first thing I saw was a guy with blond hair dressed in gold lame trunks. I did not know that he was dressed as "Rocky" from the movie. My reaction was what is this?

TD - How did you react to that experience?

MW - By time the night was done, my roommate and I were so struck by what we had seen that we found a reel to reel tape tape of the soundtrack and wrote down lyrics so we could sing along.

TD - What about your participation as a cast member?

MW - I've been in seven casts, and played, at one point, every part but Trixie. (most of my casts did not perform it). Nowadays I do the Criminologist, or Dr. Scott..

TD - Did you continue to be in casts?

MW - Yes. Cast 6 and 7 are the Austin casts...O'Brien's Orchestra (cast 7) and Queries (cast 6). They are the most gifted casts I've been part of. There are follow spots, a stage manager, and an archive of call back scripts going back to the 70's, It's on the very young side. We had one cast member that was 15 who performed with their dad's permission and attendance. The cast is very engaged in blocking their positions and saying their lines.

Of the other five casts, two (casts 4 and 5) were in El Paso. By comparison, they were not very well organized.

You could do a walk on in street clothes.

Casts 1-2-3- were in the Quad Cities area. Of those, Davenport and Rock Island were the biggest.

TD - Have you been a non-stop cast member, or hav eoyu taken a break from it?

MW - My work took me away from participating as a cast member for about eighteen years. When I came back to playing in a cast, I was amazed at the difference 18 years made. The O'Brien's Orchestra cast cast now the most organized versus the come as you are in El Paso. In the early days, none of casts had a cast name, or a supply of costumes, or tech equipment to put on a production.

TD - What are some example of the different casts?

MW - My first three casts, Iowa and Illinois, we were (a) lucky to have a full cast (we did sometimes do double parts, and not just Eddie and Scott!), and (b) not equipped with costumes, props or technical support equipment. Screen Accurate? Not even. But we tried.

By the time I joined the El Paso cast number 4 performing at a dollar theater near my house – we were as challenged as my first three – meaning tough to get a full cast in costume. And I was about twice as old as my cast mates! Think that's probably when I inherited the pretty much permanent parts of Crim and Scott, plus pre-show. Whatever the lack, we made up for in heart. El Paso (cast number 4) managed to get thrown out of every 24 hour diner in the town (since we came in costume, you can just envision that!).

El Paso cast number 5 performed at the theater in Cielo Vista mall (think that may be gone – but it is close to the WalMart where the El Paso shooting happened), we could count on a full cast, mostly in appropriate costume. Casual props, but no tech equipment.

TD - Did you notice any cast you were in that really stood out?

MW - Yes, when I joined "Queerios" after the 18 year hiatus. The cast OWNS two $500 follow spots, has a stage with two built in cutouts – one flips up to be the jukebox and the other the back of the throne where Frank throws his cape – a full set of cast costumes – a light control deck and light box to rig a theater as necessary - and even a supporting website.

And now, "O'Brien's Orchestra" – renamed because of some … friction … along the way with "Queerios" leadership. We inherited all the equipment and props and tech gear.

TD - Does the cast have merch?

MW - Yes, we have merch… so to speak. We have screen printed T-Shirts ("Rocky Horror Slut"), buttons, and prop bags. We do actively discourage (at request of theater) anyone bringing their own prop bags. Haven't seen rice or squirt guns in AGES. And lighters are out in favor of glow sticks, which we put in the prop bags.

As you can see, there's been quite a bit of evolution along the way.

TD - What else have you noticed that's new to you after your eighteen year break?

MW - Physical contact among cast members has changed quite a bit, getting a little bit more professional. At "put your hands on your hips" from "Time Warp", people got possibly too familiar in the earlier days. And, the de-virginizing has become less raucous.

TD - What about the growth of the audience?

MW - I've seen "Rocky Horror" become multi-generational. My daughter has been (is now) in a cast. Our two kids saw the movie when they were 18. (see daughter Becca Walsh's interview *"Oh God, my dad's wearing fishnets and heels…"*).

I know people who met as cast members and got married.

TD - How would you sum up the "Rocky Horror" phenomena?

MW - It has never stopped, after over 45 years. "Rocky Horror renews itself…18 year-olds today are the new audience. There are always newcomers to the "Rocky Horror" experience.

3. Lisa Sutton - Dad: "I'm NOT taking you to see THAT!" Lisa: That made me decide "Now I have to see it!"

TD - What was your first awareness of "Rocky Horror"?

LS - I grew up in Los Angeles, and my first exposure to "The Rocky Horror Picture Show" was when I saw the trailer at the UA Westwood before it opened. I was at a movie with my father, who must have seem my eyes pop out of my head as the trailer played, because he leaned in to me and said "I'm NOT taking you to see THAT!" That made me decide "now I have to see it!" I managed to make it on my own...a few hundred times over the next few years. It was electric, struck me the moment I saw the trailer.

TD - Once you saw the movie, what was your reaction?

LS - My friends went to see it. They sang the songs. I went a few months later at the UA Westwood. I went again the next night with another friend. The movie was not yet playing at midnight.

TD- Did you like it?

LS - It exploded in my head. I noticed things I had not noticed before. I started figuring it out. I watched it a second time in a row that day. The next morning I went to Westwood Sunday morning, looking for the soundtrack, but could not find it. I wanted to hear the music again. I found the Roxy cast album and the English album that day.

TD - Tell me about your Tiffany experience - the first theater in LA to show it at midnight.

LS - After the UA Westwood stopped playing he movie, I started hearing about the Tiffany theater on the Sunset Strip. Everything changed for me. I saw the Tim Curry " Read My Lips" show at the Roxy in the summer of 1978. The movie was growing. I went and spent the night in front of the Roxy. I was so blown away how many people were there in front of the Roxy. Someone I met there took me to the Tiffany.

TD - Can you sum up the experience of seeing Rocky Horror at midnight at the Tiffany?

LS - The next couple of years the Tiffany became complete pandemonium. It was just crazy watching it go form 0 to 60 in just a couple of years.

TD - What about the friends you met at the Tiffany?

LS - I had the fun of discovering you could make people laugh if you said the right thing. Dressing up was fun. At theTiffany, I started meeting people dressed as transvestites, and could not tell if it was a man or woman. But, not thinking it through too much. I was meeting an intense diversity of people. It became a community that I was part of. We all became family. The bond was to make a costume and get dressed up. A community started to build around it. Something about it felt "this was mine". Nobody at school was talking about it. It was a little place to go, my little piece of the world.

TD - Did you take part in the audience participation?

LS - Yes, we started performing, and became just part of the ritual— It was 24/7 Rocky Horror as the center of my life. Part of it was the movie, but it really ended up as the community…as our place, our thing. The most important was that it was my time and my place.

TD - Did you consider the Tiffany to be a "home" for you?

LS - It was growing and happening all over the country. The Tiffany was the Los Angeles hub, until it closed and the Nuart became the home for the midnight show. Eventually, everything being done anywhere else wound up at the Tiffany. Over time, the real draw was hanging out in the lobby, meeting with friends, darting into the auditorium at certain points. It grew and evolved.

TD - How did dressing up make you feel?

LS - One night, when I went to buy my ticket, which you had to do at least an hour before the show or you could not get a ticket, the new Tiffany manager saw that we were dressed in 50's prom dresses as Eddie's groupies. She said "be my guest and sit in the front row." That was such a feeling of being special.

TD - Dd you become a fixture at the Tiffany?

LS - Yes. Going to the movie at midnight, hanging out after midnight, hanging out with exotic people, being treated like we were special. In two to three years at the Tiffany every weekend, I became a star within the theater. It was just such a unique experience. Me, a teenage girl making minimum wage at a coffee shop.

TD - Was there any merch at that time?

LS - No. It was DIY. I made buttons and shirts and sold them at the theatre. There was no Rocky Horror merchandise. Just a promo t-shirt. People were selling Rocky rice and making their own stuff to fit the demand for merchandise.

TD - What's your lasting memory of the Tiffany?

LS - It was a crazy party environment. That was in the late 70's, people just having fun hanging out outside the theatre. There was a "Rocky Horror" sidewalk scene. The more we came, the more we became part of the scenery.

4. Sal Starts a Fan Club

An Interview with Sal Piro - Founder and President of "The Rocky Horror Picture Show" Fan Club

TD - Not long after "The Rocky Horror Picture Show" opened at midnight at the Waverly Theater in Greenwich Village (April 2, 1976), I got a call at Fox from Sal Piro, who told me had been a seminary student and then taught in Catholic Schools for 3 years. He was already in New York City and looking to be an actor or comic. "That career was put aside", he told me, "because 'The Rocky Horror Picture Show' came into my life". He wanted to know "Do you have a 'Rocky Horror' fan club?". We did not, and at Sal's urging to consider it, I said I would get back to him.

When I called Lou Adler for his thoughts, he encouraged having a fan club but he suggested, "keep it on the mom and pop level…let it be driven from the street, not from the studio". While the studio fully supported Sal and his plans, and I was always available to Sal,

Fox never interfered with what he wanted to do. The grassroots organization that Sal started gradually grew into a national fan club that would eventually have international connections.

My marketing policy for "Rocky Horror" of relying on "discovery" and word-of-mouth, not paid advertising, to create awareness for "Rocky Horror" dovetailed perfectly by having a "street level" and authentic passion from the fans themselves, who have sustained the movie for almost five decades.

There could be no substitute for what Sal did for "Rocky Horror" with the Fan Cub. The movie would never have reached the status of the longest continuously running movie in history without Sal Piro and the "Rocky Horror" Fan Club, and all of the loyal fans around the country.

TD: Could there have been a better place for the premiere of the midnight show of "Rocky Horror" than Greenwich Village?

SP: No. Playing "Rocky Horror Picture Show" in Greenwich Village at midnight (at the Waverly Theater) made sense because of the transvestite issue. "Rocky Horror" was seen as very attractive to the gay audience, and TV's came out for it right away. This was the perfect place for "Rocky Horror" to premiere at midnight.

TD: What have been your impressions of "Rocky Horror"?

SP: I found out about the movie from one of my gay friends. It was a very big gay crowd, a Village crowd, with a mostly white audience. Over the years, people loved the music, characters , and what was happening in the theaters. It didn't matter if you were gay or straight. The audience became more straight as the years went on.

Men were dressing as Dr. Frank 'N Furter, in fishnets, a corset and heels and turning their girlfriends on.

TD: Do you notice any differences between the fans circa 1975 and today's fans?

SP: The audience and fans have become more diverse. In 1980, the movie "Fame" used me and the 8th Street Playhouse cast to play ourselves...because Alan Parker when casting the kids from The School of Performing Arts...many mentioned "Rocky Horror Picture Show" as something they were obsessed with..so he wrote a whole "Rocky Horror" section into the film...because "Fame" was an urban film with a multi-ethnic cast..the audience got exposure to the ROCKY phenomenon and started going to see it at midnight showings..this certainly added to the love for "Rocky Horror" and it was no longer a mostly white audience...suddenly the audience was more ethnic, including blacks and hispanics.

Now, over 40 plus years later, the audience is a totally mixed crowd, ethnically, and both gay and straight, wherever 'Rocky Horror' plays.

TD: Any observations about multiple generations of fans?

SP: While we were going through the first year of "Rocky Horror", I saw a mother with two teens, they heard about "Rocky Horror". There was a girl and her mother-the girl played as "Magenta". They had been Kiss fans, but crossed over to Rocky Horror.

At the 8th Street Playhouse, we had a children''s workshop-they came with their parents. They were 10 and 11 years old, playing the characters. This showed that "Rocky Horror" attracted so many different ages and backgrounds.

I got letters over the years that would say "Oh, Sal, thanks for what you did with the fan club-now my grandchildren are going to see it."

TD: What have been the differences and similarities of fan experience over the decades?

SP: There are not that many differences-there are more similarities than differences, because "Rocky Horror" leads fans in a certain direction with its themes of sexual freedom-the liberating slogan of "*don't dream it be it*". It's amazing how kids and adults are in sync with each other. What kind of lines they shout at different theaters. If you couldn't dress up, you could participate by shouting out lines to the screen and be making it a live experience for yourself. I began to notice one of the reasons everyone became so close is they shared the movie in a similar way.

TD: How close do the fans get to the movie?

SP: They live the movie, they didn't dream it, they *are* it.

I was living out a fantasy, getting up on stage and acting out something. I was not on the screen, I was in front of it. That was cool enough.

TD: What about the evolution of the Fan Club?

SP The original group of us in the floor show formed a real bond at the Waverly. Me, Larry Forer, who was my vice president, and Dori Hartley, a beloved cast member whose portrayal of Frank 'N Furter caused much excitement to the Waverly/New York Fans. We found ourselves during the week spending time together, hanging out together, coming up with ideas about what we would do with "Rocky Horror" the next week.

My pre-teen sister, Lillias, was too young to be part of the group, but came along as the generations expanded. After I exposed her to "Rocky Horror" a few years later she was our leading "Magenta.

We wanted to have a fan convention, but needed an organization to back it up, so we needed a fan club. We were 19-21 years old, some were 16. I was the oldest at 26-27, and had experience as a teacher, so everyone said Sal, you be the president!

We started the "Transylvanian", with a subscription of $7 per year. Within a week, we had a check from Australia.

We had no experience, but decided we wanted the fan club to give information to fans, in a non-profit way. A fan club that was for free, providing information to fans about when and where the next conventions would be, and providing pictures, as an information society. It was very important to keep getting information out to the fans. When the internet came, it was really amazing what happened with "Rocky Horror". It suddenly became much easier to get the word out, and the evolution of the internet made it correct to use the internet to keep the fan club alive and free.

Eventually, Lou Adler was giving a certain respect to the fan club, because "Rocky Horror" fans were popping up in so many theaters around the country. For the Tenth Anniversary (held at the Beacon Theater in New York), Lou let me plan the show, and run the publicity role that was getting word out to other casts and fan groups.

TD: What is the importance of Fan Club Conventions to building community?

SP: There were different conventions during the years that were run by different people. The importance of the conventions was that they really increased the community of "Rocky Horror" fans. Lots of fans felt their world was just in their theatre. But, by coming to a convention, they saw that they shared the experience together with the fans from other cities.

Fan conventions made people strong and it was good for them to get together. Sometimes, they would meet the stars and it made these kids crazy-they would go out of their mind. I loved the conventions and anniversaries-they really kept the community going.

TD: Is there any end in sight?

SP: The fans have supported "Rocky Horror" for over 45 years (in 2021). Who says they will not be there for as long as "Rocky Horror" lives?

5. Larry Viezel - "I kind of knew there were a bunch of weirdos, my people, but I didn't know much about the experience."

[Larry has succeeded Sal as President and Manager of the Fan Club, with Sal's mentoring].

Early Experience as a Fan + The parallel existence of shadow casts and the fan club began to grow.

LV-I went with a friend, who wanted to take a virgin. This was on July 4th, 1992, at Cinema 35 in Paramus, New Jersey. I still have friends from that early show era.

I kind of knew there were a bunch of weirdos, my people, but I didn't know much about the experience. I had no expectations about what was going to happen. They called me out as a "virgin". I thought the shout out lines were very clever, but also thought that going once was enough, until the next weekend when I decided to go again. My connection with "Rocky Horror Picture Show" (now 27 years) spiraled from there.

I was obsessed after that - this was the summer of my senior year of high school, I went every Saturday night. There were no midnight shows in Albany, NY, where I was going to college, so I came home every few weeks to reconnect with the show and my fiends there, and eventually joined the shadow cast, as "Eddie". I started collecting Rocky Horror memorabilia, particularly 8x10 photos.

My first convention was a "mini-convention" in Washington DC in March 1993. I went as "Eddie", for the first time, and won the costume contest, so I started performing as "Eddie", and was performing that role in the Paramus shadow cast pretty often.

After the Washington convention, I thought I could do a better convention. I was 18 but ambitious and no one told me not to do it. I ran it and it was successful. I booked the film, and sold tickets. Lots of people showed up, and I was able to sell out the whole auditorium. Shadow casts from as far away as New Mexico came to Albany. I ran conventions in Albany from 1994 through 1996.

After graduating I came back to New Jersey. The person running "The Seduction Production" cast in Paramus wanted to retire so he handed the reins over to me. I ran another convention, this time in New York City, in 1998.

Meeting Sal

There was very little oversight of the shadow casts—we were like independent contractor types. At that time (circa 1990's) the line between the shadow cast and the audience was blurred. The fan club was a independent of the shadow casts.

I met Sal Piro, the president of the fan club, and also from New Jersey. This was at the mini-convention in Washington DC. He suggested that I join the fan club.

Sal came to two of my conventions in Albany, and I saw him again at the 1995 convention (for the 20th anniversary of the movie's release) in Los Angeles, at the Pantages Theater.

The parallel existence of shadow casts and the fan club began to grow. Between the 15th and 20th anniversaries (1990 and 1995) was the rise of the shadow casts. Up until then, the movie theaters were central to keeping the screenings going. Closer to 25th anniversary (2000), the shadow casts became organized. and the in-theater experience—still the best way to experience "Rocky Horror Picture

Show" Horror—was focused away from audience interaction toward shadow casts leading the show. Shadow casts are stronger today than ever.

On the internet

The internet started making more people aware of "Rocky Horror Picture Show", and there is now huge online community. In the early 1990's, when the internet was just starting, lots of people were getting to know "Rocky Horror" through internet "usenet" groups— a primitive system of posting messages and replies on the internet that has the effect of creating a "discussion". Today "Rocky Horror" fandom has a presence on every social media platform and on several websites.

The internet both helped and hindered. The advantage was that all of a sudden there was communication between all markets - you could instantly communicate with other "Rocky Horror" fans around the world. But the eventual effect was that you were put into a silo that was just "Rocky Horror", where at the shows it used to be different fandoms conglomerating, creating a more diverse community.

As the internet grew much more sophisticated, you no longer had to go every weekend to the theater for the "Rocky Horror" experience—you could hop onto the internet and be part of the experience when you couldn't get to the theater and see the movie an the shadow cast performance, which is why the in-theater experience continues to be such an important part of the total "Rocky Horror" experience today.

6. Tony Pazuzu -"What a freaking buzz!"

TP-"What a freaking buzz! When I was 18 years old, I flew from Australia to Los Angeles to attend the 15th anniversary at Fox Studios, which was my first Rocky Con and my first time overseas.

Needless to say the impact of that experience was colossal, and still remains amongst my most memorable "Rocky" moments. It was a "Rocky" experience yet to be rivaled!

I mean, this party had EVERYTHING; the ideal venue, an unprecedented amount of original film stars in attendance, the sensational live pre-shows, musical numbers and discussions from the original cast, the mock recreation of the Waverly theatre, not to mention the sheer size of the movie screen! I just remember the crowd was a tidal wave of electricity.

Even the small touches, like the "Rocky Horror" images projected on huge walls all over the studio lot, the gift bags, the surrounding media frenzy, all the new merchandising, the impending VHS release, a new CD/Cassette box set containing audio tracks we never dreamed we'd get to hear, the Mayor of LA proclaiming it "Rocky Horror Day".

My association with this monster has been long and varied. I have been an active fan since the mid-1980s, having essentially grown up attending regular midnight screenings for many, many years here in Oz. During those early years after first discovering the film, I was an active member of my local theatre's audience participation cast, and, despite ultimately moving on from being part of the core performing group, I have continued to attend screenings semi-regularly remain an active member of the "Rocky" global community.

This life-long involvement with the fandom continues to bring me a great deal of happiness, some amazing friendships, and some truly incredible experiences. I still frequently engage with many long-term former regulars from the "Rocky Horror" days at the Waverly/8th Street Playhouse etc.

Incidentally, the live stage show continues to remain a hugely successful major theatrical event over here, being revived professionally every few years. I have attended every production mounted in Australia since 1984, with the most recent staging winding up late last year.

7. James Lajer and Joanna Stephens - "The midnight show of 'The Rocky Horror Picture Show' was where people found their community."

James: I became hooked on "Rocky Horror" thirty-seven years ago, as a fellow "outcast". Five years after attending my first midnight show, I married Joanna, also a "Rocky Horror" fan.

Because I wore a three-piece suit, to play the Criminologist, moviegoers often thought I was part of the theater management and directed questions to me. That didn't faze me at all. I liked being part of the "weirdness".

We both became players in the "Queerios" fan group in Austin.

Joanna: - As far as performing goes, James has played every part (including Trixie once), and in Austin I have played Magenta, Dr. Scott and the Criminologist.

James and Joanna speaking together:

Austin is the second longest running market in America. "Rocky Horror" was playing at the Riverside Twin from 1976 to 1983, when it became a Spanish Baptist church. It then moved to the Northcross for 14 yeas, and also played the Riverside, which closed and reopened.

A very special highlight of our "Rocky Horror" life was the visit to Austin by Tim Curry and Richard O'Brien. The keys to the City of Austin were given to them by the Mayor, who was dressed in a Mr. Peanuts mask. He wasn't a member of the cast. He just was getting into the spirit for the occasion. Tim and Richard were made honorary citizens of Austin.

Joanna: For many years, I contributed writings to the Queerios website http://www.austinrocky.org/index.php, but Shawn McHorse created and ran it. It's now dormant, but still exists as a very thorough and comprehensive archive of "Rocky Horror" history in Austin.

James and Joanna: The fan group today is called "O'Brien's Orchestra" which came as a result of organic changes. It was a changing of the guard type of thing. New faces ands new names as the cast personal evolved. The group has gone through many names for many reasons with various names.

James and Joanna speaking together: Austin is the second the longest running market in America. "Rocky Horror" was playing at the Riverside Twin from 1976 to 1983, when it became a Spanish Baptist church. It then moved to the Northcross for 14 years, and also played at the Riverside, which closed and reopened.

James: The midnight shows of "The Rocky Horror Picture Show" were where people found their community. Tim, what you helped to create was a place for people to go and be accepted when they had nowhere else to go. I have always wanted to ask Richard O'Brien how many people he saved. You are part of that because you helped save a movie that saved others. For this all I can say to you and Richard, from myself and a whole lot of other people, is thank you.

Richard O'Brien: What a truly wonderful, added, bonus this is to what is, essentially, a juvenile, musical comedy. Love, Richard

8. "What the hell did I just watch?"

Interview with MK Brown and Brett Mourglia

BM- I watched movies like "Muppet Treasure Island", "Clue", and "Home Alone 2" when I was young, and grew to love Tim Curry. He was one of the first actors whose name I committed to memory as child. In middle school I saw the DVD cover with Tim Curry sitting in the lips at Blockbuster so I rented the movie and watched it. When it was over I thought "What the hell did I just watch?" I heard of its reputation, so I did my research, read about the film making fun of B movies and old school Sci-Fi and watched it again and I fell in love with it immediately!

I went with friends to the midnight show in Houston, back when they were "The Beautiful Creatures", dressed as Dr. Scott. The guy playing Dr. Scott that night pulled me from the audience and asked me onstage to perform that role. That solidified my want to join a shadowcast.

I moved to Austin and shortly after, joined the O'Brien's Orchestra cast, and have loved it ever since. It means the world to me being able to perform one of my favorite movies on a regular basis.

The "Rocky Horror" environment is so enriching. It's the best side of being weird. The theme of "don't dream it, be it" is very moving. People that have never acted are having fun, living the dream, and just being themselves.

Each of us knows how to do each position of the technical work on our cast. Our cast can play multiple roles. We're just a group of volunteers. We are very lucky to have a very talented cast.

MK Brown interview

MK-I was nine years old the first time I saw "The Rocky Horror Picture Show". I had been out on Halloween trick-or-treating. When I got home, my Mom was watching it on TV and urged me to sit and watch it with her.

I was hooked. I watched the show obsessively. I was in love with Richard O'Brien, the hero of weirdness and non-conformity. I grew up as a queer person, and "Rocky Horror" can show what I feel inside. I've loved it ever since I was a kid. For my high school graduation I decorated my cap with fishnets and gold glitter that spelled out "Don't Dream It! Be It!"

I always wanted to be a performer. I was quiet and shy and it gave me a way to put myself out there. I went to college in Montana…there were no "Rocky Horror" casts or showings. I joined the cast after college. It's been absolutely fantastic. It made me a better person. I met my partner (Brett) doing "Rocky Horror". This cast has given me more than I could have ever imagined.

The movie is now at the Alamo Draft House Village - we are the second longest running cast in the country.

We are currently the O'Briens' Orchestra. Prior to that (4 years ago), the former cast was called "Queerios".

We had a fantastic couple of cast directors when we became O'Briens Orchestra who were able to build us a very strong foundation.

We just had a show in San Antonio, at the Aztec Theater showing "Rocky Horror". It was a full house.

MK and Brett together

When the movie went onto video and you could rent or buy it, the fact is it made more people excited to want to come to the theater to see the shadow cast. They have heard about what we do and it makes them want to come for the experience. The video is good P.R. for us.

Fandom is a whole different ball game. There are many "Rocky Horror" cyber communities, and lots of "Rocky Horror" shadow cast groups. When we travel, we try to find a show and see those casts. People from other parts of Texas come and perform with us. It's a community of shadow casters going together. It's a really beautiful thing.

There are Facebook groups that cover all aspects of RH.

We have become more modern and more polished. The shadow cast has been an incredible tool to interact with other acts, getting costumes information, for example. It has opened a whole new world with the stage show. Even on YouTube you can watch clip of what's happening with "Rocky Horror" in other places.

A Frank N'Furter in the UK named David Bedella 2006-2010 is sort of a cult within the cult. He's our favorite. The Austin shadow cast looks to that production to find inspiration.

Once a year we do a Rocky-fest. Just in Austin, where we get around the movie by showing scenes and clips and play the audio. It's really fantastic. For example, we use the Broadway version of "Science Fiction". Comedians and drag performers do sets between our scenes.

9. Kristian Fletcher and "Cards 4 Sorrow" in Brisbane, Australia. "I was very inspired by the American 'Rocky Horror' cult".

In October 2000, aged 17, Kristian Fletcher began presenting screenings of "The Rocky Horror Picture Show" with a floorshow by local fan group Cards 4 Sorrow. It was "Rocky Horror" which gave Kristian the interest and experience to present other themed cult movie events and he expanded with Able Productions in 2003. He's now one of the key people at the forefront of Brisbane's now-flourishing cult/classic cinema scene. Director John Waters has said that "Kristian Fletcher is like an ambassador of cult movies"

TD - Do you remember the first time you connected with "Rocky Horror"?

KF - Yes, it was in 1997, when I was 14 years old. I went on a family road trip over two states and prior to leaving, a RH obsessed friend did a copy of the 21st anniversary soundtrack on cassette. Going in blind, I played the cassette on repeat in the car and - having not seen the movie - pieced together what I believed was going on in the movie. Even then, hearing the haunting 'Science Fiction' gave me goosebumps

TD - And, what about the first time you saw the movie?

KF - I discovered the movie in high school through friends. I watched it once in 1997 and it really didn't grab my interest. For the next two years, I would hear references to the movie and was curious to re-visit. A friend lent me the VHS and I was very inspired by the American RH cult - via early websites, fanzines, VHS special features. In Australia, audience participation is very influenced by the US.

TD - After the "re-visit" you became a fan?

KF - Yes. Cosmos Factory was a godsend. I would spend my afternoons trawling through everything I could read, wishing to learn everything I could about RH.

TD- What did that lead to?

KF - One Sunday in early 2000, I walked the streets of Brisbane with a petition, asking people to sign "I would love to see Rocky Horror at the cinema"

With a petition of a few pages, I approached some cinema chains about running the movie and they weren't interested. The funny thing is, those same venues are now screening the movie three times a year. Perhaps venues don't like encouraging the shadowcast element and audience participation due to the mess it creates.

Schonell Theatre sent a reply letter (I'd forgotten I had written them earlier) to say they'd love to trial a screening – that ended up being 20 October 2000 – the first time Cards 4 Sorrow performed the full floorshow alongside a screening. Back then it was even on 35mm print (as this print had been well used, it would often skip parts of the movie, throwing the cast into disarray and confusion) But the show had to keep going.

Once we knew we had a screening booked in and months to plan, I went about trying to put Cards 4 Sorrow together. We had a couple of meetings with core people I had found and put the word out via posters at universities and drama groups. The problem with doing this – interest is high but once theatre students realise it's lip-synch, the interest dies down. Our first rehearsal in July 2000 had almost 30 Transylvanians – which was 6 by the following week! We rehearsed on Sundays in the lead up, whilst costumes were made and props put together.

Nowadays, we don't rehearse. It's assumed everyone who has played those parts before can step in at any time and do these again. It has made it hard when audiences think they are attending a STAGE PRODUCTION (even though all promotion says it's the movie with shadowcast) so they are expecting the cast to be as polished as possible.

In the lead up to our first show, the disused Boggo Road Gaol organisers asked us to perform a couple of the songs during their outdoor screening in September 2000. We were rough, there was no lighting, and for Frank's cape – I just grabbed an old red curtain from home to drape around Trevor Holland who was playing Frank N Furter

(Trevor Holland and myself are the only people who have been there since the very beginning and still perform with the cast)

I started off as Riff Raff but after trying out Brad in 2003, I have played the part ever since.

Whilst I should have been concentrating on my teachers degree at university, I was setting up "Cards 4 Sorrow"

TD - Where did the cast name 'Cards 4 Sorrow' come from?

KF - Most shadow casts are named from a reference in the movie. I called us 'Cards 4 Sorrow' which is mentioned in the song "I'm Going Home" by Richard O'Brien

"Everywhere it's been the same, feeling

Like I'm outside in the rain, wheeling

Free, to try and find a game, dealing

Cards for sorrow, cards for pain"

TD - Are cast members theater arts students, fans, trained, or just spontaneous?

KF - We began as theatre kids, but it's now more RH fanatics who have a creative side. Most cast hold what they deem 'everyday jobs' so - like RH has always been - this is an outlet to let your hair down every couple of month

TD - Are your shows at midnight

KF - We've never done a midnight screening. Midnight movies aren't really part of Australian culture. We often joke that the public transport system isn't good enough to allow us to screen at midnight (getting audiences there and out would be difficult). Our screenings take place at 8pm now and this works well.

TD - Are the shows both weekend nights?

KF - I've had over 20 years to trial ways of hosting the screenings, and Saturday night screenings always bomb, hence only showing RH on Friday nights.

TD - How often does RHPS play in Brisbane, or are your shows special engagements

KF - We originally screened once every 2 months and found it was no longer a 'special event'. Audiences declined and we found demand was the way to ensure all screenings are sell outs and have the energy in the room to give the full RHPS experience. There's nothing worse than a full interactive RHPS screening with 30 people in the audience. The cast feed off the audience energy

TD - What's the audience participation like?

KF - Audience participation is still hit and miss in Australia. Audience members will tell others to be quiet because they are ruining the movie experience. As a lot of the lines are less known nowadays, there is usually one main person who will yell, sometimes resulting in them being seen as obnoxious.

TD - What has been the effect of the movie in Australia generally?

KF - After an initial premiere down south, Fox had trouble finding venues that were interested in screening the movie. It opened in 1976 at the Valley Twin (later Globe Theatre) and would play twice or three times a day.

TD - What about the stage play?

KF - The original Australian productions were popular due to famous cast members (Reg Livermore, Russell Crowe) The shows were presented in their raw format which reflected the stage shows origins. Even before the movie was released here, the Usherette would throw Mars Bars out into the audience during

"Science Fiction". The audience participation elements were there long before the movie took off here.

The stage production was here in 2014 and 2018 for the anniversary tour. Modern incarnations of the stage show rely too much on the movie imagery and the show has unfortunately lost its low-budget charm originally evident in the 1970s productions.

TD - What are your observations from being part of the RH phenomena for so many years?

KF - It's become cross generational – people who were fanatics in the early days are now bringing their [children to share the experience with them].

TD - What Impact does the floorshow have versus a regular screening of the movie?

KF - A lot of cinemas now screen the movie regularly, sans floorshow. In early 2000 when I approached theatre chains about bringing the movie back, they weren't interested. These are the same cinemas now screening the movie every Halloween and sporadically throughout the year. But the ultimate experience in with floorshow so we find a lot of people hold off and attend ours as its the entire package.

TD - What about other Australian cities?

KF - There is a cast in Melbourne - 'Pelvic Thrusts'. The Sydney cast 'Fun In the Dark' ran for a long time but ceased a few years back. I find a lot of cast members grow out of being involved. As we only perform every couple of months, it's not too hard to commit. If we were doing it weekly, the audience and cast interest would decline significantly.

Some New Zealand fans attended one of our screenings at Globe Theatre and were so inspired, they started up their own cast called Hot & Flustered.

TD - How has the fan experience changed over the twenty plus years of your involvement with RH?

KF -Today, fans are met around the world via the Internet and social media. In 1999, when I started the Australian RH Fan Club, there was posters in shops, listings in places I could get it listed – definitely harder than spreading the word via social media and actually reaching your target audience

TD- Tell me about the Fan Club that you started.

KF - I didn't have internet access at home so I would book one hour on the computers at the local library and trawl through newsgroups and fan sites to indulge in everything RH related.

Every three months, a printed newsletter which, by the time was reached, was most likely old news. I had my own PO Box and was even listed in the Yellow Pages (some of the odd phone calls I would receive from drunk people making RH references) By 2003, the fan club was dissolved with no announcement. In the age of social media, finding fans is as simple as a click of a mouse so fan clubs almost become irrelevant. Fans are now connected to news and updates immediately.

TD - What about Conventions?

KF - On Friday the 13th September 2002, I presented the first Australian Rocky Horror Convention at Boggo Road Gaol. We had Games, a Best Dressed fashion show, Karaoke room and more. The local news broadcasted the weather from the events and members of Cards 4 Sorrow featured dancing to the Time Warp

George Sourris, who ran RHPS at Valley Twin, was a special guest for the night and 'cut the ribbon' to officially open the convention. I learnt a lot about publicity and event coordination from running the Rocky Horror Down Under convention. Skills which I took with me into the future.

The promotion machine began three months prior and I ensured we were featured in as many media outlets as possible. We had interstate visitors.

This was in the early years of the internet in Australia so pre-online bookings patrons would purchase their tickets via mail.

The convention culminated in a screening of RH with Cards 4 Sorrow floorshow followed by Shock Treatment. 120 people attended the convention and 400 in total were there by the end of the night.

TD - Were there any unusual promotions?

KF - My RH memorabilia collection was doing the rounds in 2001 and on display at various council libraries around Brisbane. To complement these, Cards 4 Sorrow were invited to perform the floorshow alongside a screening at different libraries from 2001-2003.

Cards 4 Sorrow performed the full Rocky Horror Picture Show floorshow for the first time at Schonell Theatre on Friday 20 October 2000. At that stage, we wanted to get at least one screening up and running before we decided on the next chapter and how often we would perform/screen the movie going forward.

We moved into 2001 with a screening once every three months at Schonell.

Metro Arts had regular cult movie screenings from 2005 onwards including RH with Cards 4 Sorrow.

In early 2006, I was invited to bring my cult movie screenings (including RH) to the old Valley Twin cinema in Fortitude Valley, Brisbane - now named Globe Theatre. It was a thrill to perform in the actual cinema where the film ran for many years back in the late 70s. It still felt like 1976 in there! It was almost like the RH cult had come full circle, and I was the next

We didn't have a stage so backstage area was created via a black sheet run along underneath the screen. Cards 4 Sorrow performed on the carpet in front. Looking back, we had no elevation so people most likely only saw heads of cast members. But we still had a ball. At 200 capacity, it was the perfect atmosphere for RH screenings.

We continued at the venue until 2011, during which time I co-ordinated and presented several cult movie programs. I learnt a lot about film programming and distribution - knowledge which I've carried with me to this day.

We moved back to the Schonell Theatre and made that our regular home from 2012 to 2019 (we haven't performed since then due to COVID)

TD - What has been the impact of all the hard work you did for RH?

KF - Once Cards 4 Sorrow was established and going well, I realised there would be interest in OTHER cult movie screenings. In 2004, Schonell hosted my first non-Rocky Horror event - a 2-week horror movie festival which saw sell-out crowds. RHPS was included on the program alongside Little Shop of Horrors - both including floorshow performers.

I had been bitten by the bug, and this saw me branch out to other venues and commence cult movie screenings. I'm still running these screenings to this day, being now sought out for my cinema work in Brisbane and an 'infamous' name which people call on to re-energise a failing cinema.

People are nostalgic about movies of their earlier year, and often want to revisit with a group of friends, or share with the next generation. I've seen parents bring their 9 year old daughter to screenings - she is now in her twenties, a parent, and no doubt will one day bring her child along.

I've gone on to present screenings with floorshow for movies such as "Grease", "Cry Baby", "Little Shop of Horrors", "Blues Brothers", "Dirty Dancing" and "Repo The Genetic Opera", but due to the theatrical roots of RH, the film always works best as perfect fodder to be performed alongside.

TD - Has Cards 4 Sorrow ever been filmed?

KF - Yes. Cards 4 Sorrow will appear in the upcoming documentary The Rocky Horror Phenomenon which was filmed in the Globe Theatre.

TD - Do you have any final thoughts about the RH phenomenon?

KF - RH is always going to be cross-generational. Elements of the film - whether it's the music, the subject matter, or the characters - are always going to be something that people want to emulate. Brian Thomson said the film hasn't dated and I agree completely. RH is timeless.

10. The Last Word

Interview with Amy Galaudet

"What, Tim? You wrote a book about your adventures in show biz? I never knew you were even in Hollywood. Friends for 30 years, and you never mentioned it. Talk about low key—you are off the piano."

11."Hollywood didn't know what to do with 'The Rocky Horror Picture Show'," said author Vito Russo, in his landmark 1981 study of "queer cinema". (source: Vito Russo - The Celluloid Closet, pp.52-53, Harper and Row Publishers, New York 1981).

TD- But he was wrong: I was a Hollywood studio executive, and I did know what to do with it…save it from oblivion whether I liked the movie or not; many others might like it. "When Adler asked Deegan what he thought of the film, Deegan told him the truth; he didn't like it. "It wasn't to my taste, said Deegan. Surprisingly, Adler was pleased with his response. "He said now I could be objective about the film".

12.LA-"Tim Deegan was with the project from the beginning," said Executive Producer Lou Adler. "He sat on the curb with me outside the theater in Santa Barbara. The only glimmer of hope was that there were four or five people who sat through it (the disastrous sneak preview) and came up after the film and thanked us for making that kind of film. We were really happy. It was almost like we made it for someone."

13.TD- "I was totally convinced there was a midnight audience".

14-."Go ahead and try it". - Laddie

I eventually went to Laddie (Alan Ladd, Jr.), who had recently become the President of Fox, and pitched him my midnight release plan. The movie had been shelved by the studio's management and declared a "failure". By then, nobody else at the studio would even talk to me about it.

The only question he asked was how much it would make at the box-office. I had no comparisons because a studio had never done a midnight show before, but confidently replied "five-million-dollars" Laddie said "Go ahead and try it". -Tim Deegan

15. "It was great when it all began, and it still is!"

Mark Jabara

Full interview in chapter The Deep Down Under Roots of "Rocky Horror"

16. There's no crime in giving yourself over to pleasure...there is in Kalamazoo!

Matthew Jon Beck

MJB-My first introduction to the film was a still reproduced in a movie magazine that I saw upon returning from a church Halloween party in 1975.

Pretty sure I had the soundtrack LP memorized before I saw the picture - as any good musical theatre major would!

I didn't actually see the movie until 1981. My buddies left my 18th birthday party early to head over to Kalamazoo for a midnight screening. They invited me along on a Saturday night soon thereafter...and the rest is history!

17. "Cult films have been around a long time, but there's never been anything like this before," says Marc Mancini, an associate professor of film at West Los Angeles College who also teaches at USC.

MM-"What fascinates me is that it's the first real example I have seen of participatory film, where the barrier between the audience and screen is totally broken."

"For hundreds of years the theater has attempted to break down the barrier between the audience and the stage. When you come down to it, Shakespeare's soliloquies were exactly that. But that's sort of easy to do physically on the stage. A movie theater is an entirely difference space. A character on the screen cannot walk into an audience."

There wasn't any deliberate effort to structure the movie to produce the cult that's grown around it. So how did it happen? The bizarre sexual theme is part of the answer, Mancini suspects. But there have been plenty of more bizarre movies made over the years. There really isn't any answer, he says.

"I don't know that there's any particular message, except maybe that it's OK to be weird," he says. "There's an appeal to gays, bisexuals, anyone who feels outside the sexual norm of society. But it also appeals to a lot of people who just like playing the game, people who go to gay discos even though they aren't gay. You've got the whole Hollywood kinky crowd. Beverly Hills kids showing how weird they are, others who want to see what's going on."

"It's the first real example I have seen of participatory film, where the barrier between the audience and screen is totally broken.

18. "Remove those lewd, lascivious lips mouthing the words 'Twentieth Century Fox' from the 'Rocky Horror Picture Show' trailer" - Dennis Stanfill - Fox Chairman and CEO. (ie: "Twentieth Century Fox has brought you all sorts of movies, but Twentieth Century Fox has never brought you anything like 'The Rocky Horror Picture Show").

One year later…

"Star Wars" and "The Rocky Horror Picture Show" have been two of the studio's box office successes in 1976. (Stanfill to Fox executives).

19. Mike Shapiro- I'm glad they didn't ask me to make a trailer for "The Rocky Horror Picture Show"; I wouldn't know what to do with it, and I made over 500 trailers for MGM as their trailer supervisor.

20. Tony Seiniger "I wanted to create something that was sexier and a bit kinky, hence the biting lips for the poster.

21. Lorelei Shark (lips model for poster) - I was actually known for my pout! Pouting gives lips a fuller appearance. It's what all the models do today, but I was the only one who did it in the late 60s, early 70s.

22. Jeff Kanew (trailer maker) - I don't remember getting any specific "direction" about the RHPS trailer from Fox...they were still pretty WTF?

23. Rhea Ruggiero (actress on trailer) "The most successful spokes-mouth in movie history"

24. Jean-Louis Rubin, then the Vice President of 20th Century Fox International. - The life of "Rocky Horror'" in foreign was not very good. \We had problems throughout international markets...the notion of midnight shows did not work...the concept was totally alien...In the United States midnight was popular, but not in Europe or Japan...we just couldn't make it work.

25. "I never heard a word about 'The Rocky Horror Picture Show', which had just started its midnight run. It was always 'Star Wars'. There is a parallel with the two movies: 'The Rocky Horror Picture Show' needed to be discovered. In point of fact, so did 'Star Wars.'"

David Weitzner—Vice President of Advertising at Fox

26. "My marketing policy for "Rocky Horror" was centered on "discovery" and word-of-mouth, never using any paid advertising, to create awareness for "Rocky Horror". It dovetailed perfectly by having a "street level" and authentic passion from the fans themselves, who have sustained the movie for almost five decades".

-Tim Deegan

27. Neal Lemlein -"Looking back at the "Star Wars" campaign, I think the plan we developed was dynamic, extremely well thought out and well ahead of its time. The campaign approach we took attempted to address multiple audience segments. The plan structure resembled a classic Madison Avenue, state- of- the art marketing framework and included stated objectives. We analyzed and defined the overall target audience definition and its subsets."

Neal Lemlein—Account Executive, Doyle Dane Bernbach

28. Lani Jo Leigh -"We are the only theater in the world with this claim to fame..." Interview with Lani Jo Leigh, Owner of the Clinton Street Theater, a Portland, Oregon-based cinema.

TD-First, congratulations on playing "The Rocky Horror Picture Show" for 43 years in the same theater. I don't know of any other original theaters that can say this. Do you?

LJL - As far as I know, we are the only theater in the world with this claim to fame. "The Rocky Horror Picture Show" began its run at the Clinton St. Theater on the first weekend of April, 1978. It's screened every Saturday night since then. Even during the COVID-19 pandemic, when it played secretly to an audience of one.

TD-Let's take a look back to the beginning: how did you and the Clinton Street Theater get involved with this movie?

LJL - In the early 1970s, the Clinton St. Theater was rescued from being another in a long line of Portland "Adult" theaters by what might now be considered a "hippie" commune. This collaborative group of community organizers operated a monthly literary journal and founded a health food store and restaurant in the neighborhood. The Clinton St. Theater was yet another way to enhance the life of Portland's SE residents. "The Rocky Horror Picture Show was a good fit for the community". The film played a bit after it first opened in 1975, but in 1978 the decision was made to screen the film every Friday and Saturday night at midnight. Sometime in the 1980s, after the Clinton collaboration disbanded and the theater was again owned privately, the theater dropped the Friday night screenings, but continued to show RHPS every Saturday night.

TD-Were you influenced by the Rocky Horror Fan Club or what other theaters were doing, or did the Clinton Street experience just organically evolve?

LJL - The Clinton St. Rocky Horror experience evolved organically and is very much in keeping with life in Portland, both now and over the past 43 years.

TD-What is the name of your shadow cast and, if you took it from the movie, what's that reference?

LJL - Our shadow cast is the Clinton Street Cabaret. The name pays homage to the sense of community that surrounds our corner and neighborhood.

TD-How has you audience evolved over the decades? Have you seen the movie, that in many cities originally appealed to a LGBTQ+ audience, become a general audience movie experience?

LJL - "The Rocky Horror Picture Show" is for anyone who has ever felt like a misfit. The screening has enhanced the lives of many LGBTQ+ members of our community, but it's really the encouragement to Be Yourself, Accept Yourself that keeps people coming back.

Our screening has also become like a rite of passage for many young people in Portland, and now we have parents and even grandparents who are coming with younger family members so that they can experience something that in many ways changed their lives.

TD-What about your fan base? Has there always been a devoted following?

LJL - We have always had a devoted following. Audience members who come back week after week and cast members who perform for several years or more. RHPS is also a jumping off point for many who initially felt unsure about themselves. I've seen folks start out clueless about their identity, both sexual and otherwise, and now are pursuing graduate degrees in physics, music theory or mathematics. Some have taken up acting or producing drag shows and horror films. Somehow, being part of "Rocky Horror" makes it possible to believe that they can achieve significant goals, that however they identify, they can lead worthwhile and full lives. This is from folks who often started off depressed, anxious or suicidal. I've had many people tell me that "Rocky Horror saved my life."

TD-Have you seen two or three generations of the same family become fans of the movie?

LJL - Yes, it's always fun, especially during the off-color virgin games, to see moms and grandmas embarrassing their teenagers

TD-As this book was being written, the country suffered through a Covid pandemic that shut everything down. How did The Clinton Street Theatre deal with that?

LJL - The Clinton Street Theater was forced to close its doors on March 15, 2020. The following week, the eMCee for the 2nd and 4th Saturday BIY (Be It Yourself) nights, decided to come and watch the movie by himself. At the time we thought we would be back in six weeks. But the weeks stretched into months and then over a year, and Nathan was there every single weekend at midnight to watch the movie on the big screen. So now when we say that the movie has shown in our theater every single week since April, 1978, it's the truth!

TD-How about the impact of the home video? Do you think that helps or hurts the fan experience?

LJL - Home video only pales in comparison to what we offer at the Clinton St. Theater, whether it's the BIY nights or the weeks when the shadow cast is present. For one, who wants to clean up the mess of thrown rice and toast and playing cards. It's not a dinner party if you're the only one blowing a horn. And it would feel weird to yell callbacks at the TV screen when you're alone. The fun of "Rocky Horror" is in the collaborative experience. It's dressing up in fishnet stockings and a corset. It's in drinking a beer, laughing with friends, getting out of an insulating and sometimes deadening comfort zone. You can't challenge yourself or take risks from a living room couch, and those who come out for our interactive live experience of RHPS understand that.

TD-Is there anything gels you would like to add?

LJL - Thanks for this opportunity to participate.

29.An interview with Seth Willenson - Films, Inc. I wanted to make "The Rocky Horror Picture Show" into a big college event.

I started my career at New Line in 1970 and oversaw the release of John Water's "Pink Flamingos" and "Reefer Madness" in the early 1970's. New Line played theatrical and colleges with its movies. In the mid 70's I moved to Films Inc, which was a 16mm film distributor, with the idea of making colleges into a network of admission-charging theaters. There was almost no pay TV or home video. In fact, it was very hard to see a movie after its initial theatrical run until it went to tv syndication.

Films Inc. was the 16mm distributor for Fox, MGM and Paramount. In New York City, I had been working with Hal Sherman who invited me to a dinner-theatre presentation of "The Rocky Horror Show". Soon after that, I attended "26 For 76", that was hosted by Fox at the studio to promote upcoming releases.

I was sitting with Bill Quigley, the film buyer for the Walter Reade Organization, who had a lot of success with "Pink Flamingos" and "Reefer Madness" and he asked me if I had any midnight shows .

I told him about the "Rocky Horror Show" dinner-theater stage show that I had seen in New York. I had not seen the movie, which was not playing anywhere, having failed in LA as a standard movie and been pulled out of release. But, the play had music and crazy costumes, weirdness and an appeal to the gay audience, and I felt that it fit into the non-conformity, counterculture mood of a significant part of the country .

Films, Inc. had the 16mm rights and I wanted to make "The Rocky Horror Picture Show" into a big college event as well as tipping my theatrical friends. I also spoke to David Levy at the Key Theatre in Georgetown, D.C. and Randy Finley at the Harvard Exit Theatre in Seattle among others.

I felt it was different and would appeal to the audience and I suggested to Bill that he should call somebody at Fox and see if he could get it as a midnight show. I don't know if he ever did call, but Tim Deegan from Fox called Bill a few weeks later and pitched the midnight show to Quigley. A deal was made, and the Waverly became the first theatre in the country to play a midnight show of "The Rocky Horror Picture Show".

29. Bill Quigley -The Waverly—Where It All Began

Bill Quigley - Head Booker at the Walter Reade Organization

TD - How would you describe your theatre circuit?

BQ - We (the Walter Reade Organization) were the first— everybody would look at what we did and make decisions for their theaters.

TD - What was your role at the Walter Reade Organization?

BQ - Between 1975 and 1985, I was the film buyer at Reade. I could program theaters individually, but each one of our (Walter Reade) theaters had a distinct personality. Fox example, The Midtown midtown specialized in foreign language films. Our theaters on the east side played art and first run. Our 34th street theater played straight Hollywood. The Waverly focused on American independents, although the Waverly also played all Werner Fassbinder films.

TD - What was the booking environment like when "Rocky Horror" opened at the Waverly?

BQ - People forget, or may have never known, that in the mid-1970's, when "The Rocky Horror Picture Show" was released, films often were released in just one theatre with only a print campaign.

TD - How did that affect your business?

BQ - The Walter Reade Organization and Cinema 5 Theatres had a large number of theaters that specialized in foreign and independent films—both used to get lots of upscale film premieres.

TD - Did film critics play an outsized role in making or breaking a movie?

BQ - Movies premiering in New York were very "review dependent." New York was usually the first place in the world to premiere American movies, often in a single theatre, especially if it was considered "arty" or "specialized." Foreign language films often had their North American premiere in a single Manhattan theatre. Critics like Vincent Canby (he was the big gun for us 1969 -1990 at the New York Times – by the way, he started his film writing career at Quigley Publishing's Motion Picture Herald). Bosley Crowther at the New York Times 1940 – 1968 was important because he championed foreign films, Pauline Kael at the New

Yorker, and Andrew Sarris at the Village Voice could make or break a specialized film with a good review.

TD - So, it was common to use a single New York theatre to launch what would be a national release? Like using the Waverly and that kicked off the rest of the "Rocky Horror" bookings around the country?

BQ - Yes, After the results of a first run were in, the studios and other distributors would decide how to broaden the run in New York and then distribute the film throughout the rest of the country.

TD - Did the Waverly have a reputation and a following?

BQ - You had to find an audience for your theater. Audiences trusted my judgement at the Waverly. It was a fragile thing. Once you screw it up, you loose your audience. It was an age or repertory and revival theaters recycling old product. That type of programming is what preceded the Waverly type programming.

TD - I selected the Waverly to be the first theatre with a midnight showing of "The Rocky Horror Picture Show" because I knew, even far away in Los Angeles, that it was a theater that knew how to handle midnight shows. No studio ever tried this type of booking before, so I needed an "expert".

BQ - Success often relied on personal connections and an idea. We learned a lot doing the midnight screenings. WRO owned "The Night of the Living Dead" which was one of our first midnight movies. We also showed "The Harder They Come", Liquid Sky", "Pink Flamingos" and "El Topo" at midnight. We tried to cater to the atmosphere. We often played Fox Movietone newsreels in front of midnight shows, for fun.

TD - What's the appeal of running movies at midnight?

BQ - Midnight shows were a great way of generating incremental income for the theaters. You're operating 365 days a week, you have a high fixed cost. 80-90 percent of the business was on the weekend. At the Waverly it became a question of "how can we generate incremental revenue to drop to the bottom line?". There was a very light operating cost in running the midnight shows.

TD - Do you remember the "deal" you made with Fox to show "Rocky Horror"

BQ - It was a "80/20" deal. I made the "template" deal with Fox for how to split box office revenues on "Rocky Horror Picture Show" and it's a formula that a senior distribution executive friend of mine has said is the standard "Rocky Horror" licensing deal for midnight shows around the country, and always has been. Originally Fox wanted a 90/10 deal, meaning they got 90%. I negotiated an 80/20 to give theaters more revenue.

TD - You were at Reade in a very different time than today for the movie business. What was it like back then, as "Rocky Horror" entered the marketplace?

BQ - The first twin theatre in the US was built in the early 1960s. Multiplexing didn't really start gathering steam until the late 1970s and early 1980s. Theatre circuits that had theatres in major urban locations, especially Manhattan, fought to get "exclusivity" for their theatres with the product they played and wanted to be the only theatre playing that picture in a huge geographic area.

During this time, Radio City Music Hall grudgingly took "clearance" over "all theatres East of the Mississippi, instead of in all of North America. Broad "national releases" of films with up to one thousand prints and national media buys started with the growth of the suburban multiplexes in the late 1970s. With higher film production costs and broader "commercial" movies, distributors realized that they could use broadcast and radio media buys in addition to print campaigns to reach a large audience simultaneously and they determined that they could distribute the movies more broadly and justify the media costs.

TD - I've always wondered about how to spell it: is it "theater" or "theatre"?

BQ- Most exhibitors used the British spelling—theatre—popularized by my Grandfather in our film publications since 1915 to treat film – not movies - as a classy art form and not some pedestrian entertainment.

31. Tom Cooper - "Rocky Horror" Returns to the Sunset Strip

Interview with Tom Cooper, operator of the Tiffany Theater

TD - With the Waverly Theater midnight booking performing beyond expectations, selling out continuously for several months, the next step to building up a national platform of midnight shows for "The Rocky Horror Picture Show" was to open at midnight in Los Angeles as the west coast anchor to match New York.

We had played a regular, first-run engagement in Los Angeles at the UA Westwood, and needed something a little bit different for the midnight show. Only two theaters in Los Angeles, the NuArt in West Los Angeles and the Tiffany Theater on the fabled Sunset Strip had any semblance of a midnight show program. A long shot contender for consideration was the funky Fox Venice Theater at the bohemian-spirited beach town of Venice, on the Santa Monica Bay. It had a good repertory calendar and "Rocky Horror" would play there briefly as a non-midnight double-bill with Fox's "The Phantom of the Paradise" (1974) and other movies before I could identify the perfect Los Angeles venue, something to equal the perfect Waverly Theater in New York.

The choice came down to the NuArt and the Tiffany. Between them, Lou Adler gravitated toward the Tiffany because it was on the Sunset Strip. Lou's club, The Roxy where "The Rocky Horror Show" played very successfully, was close by on the "Strip", and Lou was excited about having the movie play in his neighborhood. So, a decision was made to try the Tiffany.

In this interview, Tom Cooper recounts some of the history of "Rocky Horror" at the Tiffany.

TD: What were the circumstances of you winding up with the first LA midnight show of "The Rocky Horror Picture Show"?

TC: A salesman from Fox called me and asked if I could play the movie. I had just signed the operating lease several weeks before, on March 16, 1977, and was planning on programming 3-D movies and classic movies and like I did at the Vagabond,–which I also operated, Eventually, the Fox sales manager for LA had to talk me into booking "Rocky Horror" with Friday and Saturday midnight shows as what the studio called a "test". The studio said I could keep 100% of the box-office during the test period if I would take the booking. I agreed because I wanted access to the Fox library of classics to book at the Vagabond. I thought I was doing Fox a favor. Turns out, they made my theater very successful, and somewhat notorious, with "Rocky Horror".

TD: How long did you play the movie?

TC: The Tiffany run lasted 3 days short of five years. The Tiffany opened "Rocky Horror" on June 10, 1977, several weeks after I took control of the theater. We played the movie until the Tiffany closed on Sunday March 13, 1983. "The Rocky Horror Picture Show" was the lat movie we played, at midnight the night before we closed the theater.

TD: Way did you end the run?

TC: I was only a leaseholder. The building owner sold the property to a developer.

TD: Did you have any competition? Were there any other theaters playing "Rocky Horror" at midnight?

TC: No. For the first three or so years of the run, the Tiffany had "clearance" from Fox, meaning no other theaters within my geographic zone could have a "Rocky Horror" playdate. The Tiffany was the exclusive engagement of "Rocky Horror" at midnight in LA during that period.

TD: Did you do anything different with the movie, say that the Waverly was not doing?

TC: We added 2am shows, due to popular demand. We also added a midnight show on Thursday nights in the summer of 1979 to keep up with the demand.

TD: What was your audience profile?

TC: Many in the audience were teens who mainly came in groups to the theater together, not dating couples. The time of night and the content of the movie caused this skew.

TD: How about the regulars and a repeat audience?

TC: There was huge audience loyalty. A repeat viewership was noticeable to me and my theater staff who befriended many of the moviegoers.

TD: Wasn't there something about the song "Superheroes" attached to your theater?

TC: Yes, Fox gave us a print with the Superheroes song ending the movie that was tested for three weekends in 1979 to gauge audience reaction before becoming the permanent ending at Tiffany.

TD: The Waverly may also have had that ending.

32.Barry Bostwick

"It's just a party Janet!"

"The rude, the crude and the unglued!!! That's what some writers have described the fans of ROCKY. I like to think more positively, that they are simply drunk, stoned and sleep deprived.

Those that attend our little church ceremony on a Friday or Saturday nite are simply looking for the hippest place to be. Surrounded by some" lifers" and some virgins but all of them just out for a party. That's what Brad says "it's just a party Janet!"

They come equipped with the need to debase the one they love…us. As we just do our job and can't fight back…but who would want to when there is so much energy and delight coming at us".

Sometimes wit and as Richard says …sometimes shit. They come with their own agenda and script and the Shadow Casts encourage the mayhem. The needs of the narcissists must be met with laughter and encouragement.

I love every demented minute of it and especially the Shadow Casts that have kept Rocky rocking all these years for no other reason than they believe in 'don't dream it, be it'! They are it and I love every single one of them".

Chapter 13
The Early Anniversaries

Celebrating the first, fifth, and tenth anniversaries of release.

The First Anniversary

Austin, Texas, like New York, is an epicenter of "The Rocky Horror Picture Show" experience. It's the second

longest continuously running midnight engagement of "Rocky Horror", just a few weeks younger than the New York City booking that began at the Waverly.

With its UTA college campus and student body and famous reputation for being a cool place, Austin may be seen as a good barometer for "Rocky Horror". It played a first-run engagement at the Varsity Theater in the fall of 1975. The first midnight show in Austin was at the Dobie Theater in early May 1976, which was just a few weeks after the Waverly ran the first midnight show. (1) "Rocky Horror" has been playing in Austin ever since.

Lou Adler remembers that, "I was calling the Dobie Theater on Mondays, speaking to a manager or box office. It was how I learned that the 45 or 50 people who attended were the same people each week. That was an early indication of what was going to happen." (2) This mirrored what I was hearing every Monday from Waverly manager Denise Borden and Sal Piro about the Waverly midnight shows: a core audience was building.

Joanna Stephens, an Austin "Rocky Horror" fan and Cast Historian for Queerios, provides a comprehensive history of "The Rocky Horror Picture Show" in her "History of Austin Rocky Horror (by Joanna Stephens) housed on the Queerrios website at http://www.austinrocky.org/history.php.

In 1991 the cast "adopted the name 'River City Rocky', which was then replaced in turn by 'Northcross Dressers', 'Lip Service', 'Conniving Vicious Little Two-Faced Brats', back to 'Northcross Dressers', and now finally to 'Queerios'. (3)

"The First Annual Birthday Party and Costume Ball, cosponsored by Presidio Theaters and the underground newspaper The Austin Sun, was held on Saturday, April 23, 1977, at the enormous, ornate Paramount Theater in downtown Austin. Tim Curry showed up and was awarded a certificate of honorary citizenship of Austin by Mayor Jeff Friedman, himself attired not in full "Rocky Horror" drag as the legend has it, but in a Jimmy Carter mask for the occasion. (Curry was also interviewed by the Austin Sun while in town.) The band Texoid played, and a costume contest was held. UT drama student Leo Lerma performed "Sweet Transvestite" with the band, and won first prize as Frank - one of Curry's corsets from the play The Rocky Horror Show. The evening's audience numbered 1,300 people". (4)

The Fifth Anniversary

For the fifth anniversary celebration, a modest affair, Lou Adler, Tim Curry and Cheech and Chong travelled to Denton, Texas for a celebration.

In "The Rocky Horror Show", "Denton" is the town where Brad Majors, Janet Weiss, Dr. Everett Von Scott, Ralph Hapschatt, and Betty Munroe lived. The castle of Dr. Frank N Furter was located "back down the road a few miles." In 1972, Richard O'Brien brought Jim Sharman his treatment for "They Came From Denton High", and together they worked it into "The Rocky Horror Show". It has been speculated that Denton was named after Denton, Texas as "The Rocky Horror Show" and "The Rocky Horror Picture Show" shared several references to the 1963 B-Movie "The Yesterday Machine" which took place in Texas. (5)

The 10th Anniversary

The atmosphere at Fox around the time of the 10th Anniversary was radically different from the pater familias style that hallmarked the Ladd administration when "Rocky Horror" first went into release. "Star Wars" had changed the prevailing family feel by making the suddenly very attractive and successful studio a target around which swam sharks like Denver oil magnate Marvin Davis and Australian media tycoon Rupert Murdoch, who each wound up an owner of the studio. Laddie had left, and I wondered what the new management environment, now led by the very corporate CEO Barry Diller, would be when I returned to Fox as the vice president of advertising just in time for a prospective tenth anniversary for "Rocky Horror".

Diller, who was known to frown on an annual holiday party for the staff, would have to approve the prospective "Rocky Horror" celebration, which he surprisingly did. The 10th Anniversary celebration, to be held at the Beacon Theater in New York, was the first time the studio participated in an anniversary party.

One morning shortly before that party, Diller called me to say, Murdoch, like CEO Stanfill earlier, had noticed the non-stop revenue for "The Rocky Horror Picture Show" on the studio's quarterly profit and loss statements and balance sheet and asked for the story behind that success, which Diller knew, and he told Murdoch about me and what I had done; it was now part of the history and institutional memory at Fox.

I knew "Rupe," as he asked the executive staff to call him, from his frequent visits to the weekly marketing meetings where he would sit with all of us deeply absorbed in his own paperwork until suddenly breaking in with a question about something we were talking about. His ability to parallel process whatever he was working on in the sheaves of papers his aides kept delivering to the conference room and what we were talking about was an indication for me of his brilliance.

In his phone call, Diller told me that Murdoch wanted to see "The Rocky Horror Picture Show" and asked me to give him a videotape copy of it to screen on his private jet when he flew to New York that afternoon. Sorry, Barry, but the movie has never been on video, I said, to which Barry replied that we own DeLuxe Labs, and I should call them and tell them to make a video copy as quickly as possible.

When I reached lab president Bud Stone, he said ok, but called back a bit later to say he had written orders never to make the movie available on video. But, the studio owner wants this, I retorted. Then get the orders cancelled, said Bud. Who wrote that order? I asked. You did, said Stone, several years ago. Of course, he had already started the high-speed duplication of the movie and was just giving me a hard time, but he actually did insist that the paper trail include a written cancellation by me of my order, which I now had to send to him by fax.

Two hours later, I appeared in Murdoch's outer office, with videotape in hand, asking to see him. His secretary buzzed him and said I was there, then sent me in. I got right to the point as I leaned over his desk to give him the videotape, and he leaned forward to accept it. I drew back slightly and said, "Rupe, this movie has never been on video, and now you have the only copy, so if I ever learn that another video copy exists, I'm coming straight to you for an explanation."

I watched his facial expression alter, but before he could say anything, I added, "I'm just trying to protect your valuable copyright." That got a broad smile, and I released the tape to him with a request that he return it to me after screening it. Later that afternoon, Diller called me to say he heard what I had told Murdoch and was fine with it and that so was Murdoch. When I got the tape back from Murdoch, I sent it to Bud Stone at the lab with a request that it be destroyed and that he send me the certificate of destruction.

The tenth anniversary was held on October 31,1985, in New York at the Beacon Theater with practically the whole cast in appearance, including Richard O'Brien, Patricia Quinn, Little Nell, Susan Sarandon, Barry Bostwick, Meatloaf, and Jonathan Adams.

This event was also when the Rocky Horror Fan Club became the officially recognized international fan club by 20th Century Fox, with Sal Piro as Fan Club president. It was a formalization of the great work Sal had done for a decade. Lou Adler and I knew how instrumental Sal had been; it was nice to see the well-deserved recognition of Sal and his program.

Billed as the Tenth Anniversary Convention, (6) the schedule of events was:

- Short films related to Rocky Horror
- Introduction of Sal Piro, Emcee
- Introduction of film stars
- Question and answer session with film stars
- Tribute to "Sweet Transvestite"
- "I'm Going Home" - Dori Hartley
- "Eddie's Teddy" - Jonathan Adams
- "Hot Patootie" - Meat Loaf

- "The Time Warp" - Richard O'Brien, Patricia Quinn, Little Nell Campbell

- Costume Contest

- Janet Weiss on "The Dating Game"

- "Little Black Dress" - Richard O'Brien and Cast

- "Science Fiction, Double Feature" - Richard O'Brien

- "The Time Warp Reprise" - Finale

- "The Rocky Horror Picture Show" with the 8th Street Players

- Mock Oscars awarded to the stars of the film.

While the tenth anniversary event was an extremely important and major event for the fans, and the start of major half-decade events to come—the 15th, hosted by Fox on the giant Stage 14, would be the greatest show ever. No longer would a videotape of the movie be so closely guarded; instead, the video version would be mass marketed and create one of the great turning points in the history of "The Rocky Horror Picture Show".

Notes:

1. http://www.austinrocky.org/history.php

2. to author 1/22/21

3. http://www.austinrocky.org/history.php

4. ibid

5. http://www.rockyhorrorwiki.org/wiki2/index.php?title=Denton

6. http://rockyhorrorwiki.org/wiki2/index.php?title=10th_Anniversary_Convention

Chapter 14
The 15th Anniversary: A Turning Point

A new direction for "Rocky Horror"

"What a freaking buzz! When I was 18 years old, I flew from Australia to Los Angeles to attend the 15th anniversary at Fox Studios, which was my first Rocky Con and my first time overseas. Needless to say, the impact of that experience was colossal and still remains amongst my most memorable "Rocky Horror" moments. It was a "Rocky" experience yet to be rivaled! I mean, this party had EVERYTHING; the ideal venue, an unprecedented amount of original film stars in attendance, the sensational live pre-shows, musical numbers and discussions from the original cast, the mock recreation of the Waverly theatre, not to mention the sheer size of the movie screen! I just remember the crowd was a tidal wave of electricity.

Even the small touches, like the "Rocky Horror" images projected on huge walls all over the studio lot, the gift bags, the surrounding media frenzy, all the new merchandising, the impending VHS release, a new CD/Cassette box set containing audio tracks we never dreamed we'd get to hear, the Mayor of LA proclaiming it "Rocky Horror Day" (1)

That's how Tony Pazuzu recalls "The Master's Affair" as the 15th Anniversary party held on a cavernous sound stage 14 at 20th Century-Fox studios on October 20, 1990.

Julie Baker O'Connor, another partygoer, told me, "I remember it so well. That was my first Rocky Con AND my first time seeing the movie! I remember the whole place yelled in unison, "Fuck You, Virgin" as it was announced by Sal Piro to the audience that I was,

189

in fact, a virgin to "The Rocky Horror Picture Show"~ Sal came up to me afterward and politely said, "That's probably the biggest Fuck You you ever got!" (2)

Fox did not do much to mark the anniversaries——that was left to Lou Adler and Sal Piro and the "Rocky Horror" Fan Club that Sal had started. Except for this one, where Fox elevated the party to a level as if it were the premiere of a big-star movie.

At the studio, my executive emphasis included building out the network of markets that would play "Rocky Horror" at midnight, minimizing expenses through my marketing plan that had become studio policy: "discovery" by moviegoers that may only know of the movie by word of mouth, having no advertising, and watching the profits grow.

A "win" for fans to have something for themselves and a financial windfall for the studio, an unpublicized third-party financier, and the other assorted producers and rights holders.

On the grand scale of what was happening at Fox with all its other releases, "Rocky Horror", at least in the first decade, was a footnote in the corporate suite, although the bottom-line oriented Fox chairman Dennis Stanfill couldn't miss the balance sheet black ink representing "Rocky Horror" net profits which were growing steadily as the movie took hold across the country, climaxing at over 200 theaters playing at midnight simultaneously.

Fox grew to have such dominance of the midnight movie time slot that it drew the attention of David Lynch, whom a mutual friend that worked at Fox introduced me to when he was looking to take "Eraserhead" (1977) to the midnight market. Lynch wanted to know if he could get some of our track of midnight theaters for his movie. It was a hard-fought battle by me against my colleagues to get the first-midnight show, and once I saw an opportunity to own the national midnight market with "The Rocky Horror Picture Show" for Fox, I felt compelled to protect that for Fox.

The big news at Fox, in the first few years of "Rocky Horror" midnight shows, was Laddie's slate of movies I was part of the marketing team for. It included the trifecta of comedy hits by Mel Brooks: "Young Frankenstein" (1974), "Silent Movie" (1976), and "High Anxiety" (1977). Richard Donner's "The Omen" (1976), "Star Wars" (1977), two gems from Paul Mazursky "Harry and Tonto" (1974) and "Next Stop Greenwich Village" (1976) and two movies in 1977 that were nominated for Best Picture Academy Awards, "Julia" and "Turning Point". "Alien" and "All That Jazz", both in 1979 when the Ladd era ended with a record that included a record seventeen Academy Award nominations or wins for movies Laddie green-lighted, just like he had green-lighted the midnight release of "Rocky Horror."

I worked on the marketing team for all of these movies as the studio's Advertising Manager and, once "Rocky Horror" hit it big, as the Director of Worldwide Advertising for Fox and eventually VP of Advertising, while also keeping a close control on what was happening with the distribution of "Rocky Horror".

When Laddie left Fox at the end of 1979, so did I. Then, in my mid-20s, I had already worked at MGM and Fox for several years and gained valuable experience in executive positions at both studios and was ready to branch out.

Laddie's time at Fox was a "Periclean Age" that I knew would be hard to follow no matter how talented the next studio management might be.

That would be evident when I returned to Fox a few years later as advertising vice president in the new Barry Diller management. It was from that executive position that I was able to involve Fox in the 10th Anniversary celebration held at the Beacon Theater in New York, the first time the studio participated in an anniversary party. That experience is covered in the "early anniversaries" chapter.

I had long left Fox for the second time when Lou and Sal started planning for the 15th anniversary, which was to be held in Los Angeles. Anticipating the 15th Anniversary, I scouted a Hollywood Hills "party house" with Lou as a possible location for the anniversary event, and there was talk of holding the party on a chartered boat that would cruise Santa Monica Bay, but ultimately Fox agreed to host the party on the huge, very historic and famous sound stage 14.

At 27,000 square feet, it was one of the largest sound stages on the studio lot. It was also the stage where the George Cukor movie "Something's Got To Give" (1962) was being filmed until its star Marilyn Monroe was fired, re-hired, and then died, leaving the movie unfinished, and a historical curiosity.

Once the venue was set, the content came into focus. A centerpiece of the 15th Anniversary celebrations would be the coming out of "The Rocky Horror Picture Show" on home video, which was a relatively new way to watch movies at home. The standard viewing lineage had been broadcast television and then cable. Home Video cassettes were now added to the mix.

The release of the movie to home video, causing what I thought would be a dilution of the midnight show experience, was the only time that Lou and I ever disagreed about how to market the movie. It cut deeply against what had been up until then, my "discovery" plan that counted on a combination of word of mouth followed by an incredible in-theatre experience among a discrete community at midnight, a cost-free, non-commercial marketing and distribution plan that had been working very effectively for the past fifteen years.

At no advertising cost to the studio or producer and a high entertainment value for the fans, the midnight show was a perfectly balanced equation. Marketers and movie studios love this type of sustained value proposition. The profits dropped immediately to the bottom line of the studio's and producer's balance sheets with nothing peeled off; a true money machine.

I used my experience with "The Fantastics" to show Lou how that off-Broadway stage play had gained a reputation and following at the Sullivan Street Playhouse in Greenwich Village, where it opened in 1960 and ran for 42 years, making it the world's longest-running musical. (3)

I saw the play as an adolescent and again as a twenty-something. It was familiar and I felt an emotional ownership interest in it. That's how I saw the "Rocky Horror" experience being for its fans and how home video may take away that special quality when it changed the viewing venue from a midnight show with audience participation to a daylight-lit living room viewing experience. I wasn't so sure that seeing "The Rocky Horror Picture Show" "with the lights on" was going to be as satisfying as the midnight in-theater community experience.

Lou, primarily fixated on revenue, was unswayed, and I told him I would publicly support whatever his plan was, but privately thought this was a marketing mistake driven solely by income projections instead of the intrinsic benefits of maintaining the midnight shows as the only way to have the "Rocky Horror" experience.

The sacrifice of midnight exclusivity with its unique experience in order to get more money, on top of the tens of millions of dollars of profits already in hand from the midnight shows and soundtrack albums and CDs, is an example of what Nobel Prize winning economist Paul Krugman calls, in the myopic race for money, the "marginal utility of money." He stated that, "Diminishing marginal utility is the common-sense notion that an extra dollar is worth a lot less in satisfaction to people with very high incomes than to those with low incomes." (4)

Understanding this theorem is a core element to understanding philanthropy. In medieval days, social responsibility was called "Noblesse oblige". Modernists use the phrase "to whom much is given, much is expected," which says the same thing.

With the home video release, "The Rocky Horror Picture Show" was no longer a virgin. The video company, CBS-Fox, was on board with Lou's plan and would eventually treat it as a major release, although possibly limited to a closed loop of fans that had an emotional connection to the movie. It was hard to predict, or even believe, that any newcomers —"virgins," as the "Rocky Horror" community called them—would suddenly want to be part of "Rocky Horror" as a living room experience. I thought it would take the waking up of lots of Brads and Janets to crack the commercial market with this speciality film.

Taking a page from Lou's "repetition" playbook, CBS/Fox could follow Lou's lucrative soundtrack sales plan of issuing re-releases with new features —repeatedly selling the same basic product over and over to the same market segment, with an "enhanced version" almost annually. It had worked lucratively for many years for Lou with the album and CDs.

How to meet with the CBS/Fox executives was a question to be resolved that summer and fall of 1990 when I worked out of Lou's Malibu office helping him plan out the 15th Anniversary logistics and events. The team included Lou, me, Howard Frank, Lou's assistant Julie Baker (O'Connor), Lou's personal publicist Paul

"Wasso" Wasserman, a legendary rock and roll publicist, Sal Piro, the president of the "Rocky Horror" fan club, and author of "Creatures of the Night" that would be released as part of the 15th anniversary celebrations, and rock and roll merchandising expert Paul Burke of Stauber Graphics, who dealt with pop culture merchandising and helped turn the Fox sound stage into a replica of a rock and roll arena-tour merchandise bazar. Over the previous few years, what little DIY merch that was available had exploded into merch as a major revenue element.

I knew that Lou traveled alone to meetings, unlike many celebrities who arrive with an entourage. And that most meetings were on his turf and terms instead of him going somewhere and waiting for others to start the meeting. And that he was most comfortable in his hillside Malibu office overlooking the ocean or at On The Rox, his private clubhouse upstairs at his Roxy nightclub on the Sunset Strip.

So, I was surprised when he said he was making plans to go to New York to meet with CBS, and even more surprised when he asked me to go with him, although a few years before, he and I went together to Paramount Pictures in New York for a pitch meeting on "All Washed Up," later called "Ladies and Gentlemen: The Fabulous Stains" (1982), with Paramount's Frank Mancuso, the executive vice-president for distribution and marketing.

My primary question to Lou about the New York trip was why are you going to them—hey, they should be coming to you. Let them get on a plane, cross the country, get a hotel, rent a car, and show they are taking the time and trouble, jet lag, and expense of coming to solicit you, and you then maintain the upper hand. In my mind, I thought. "You're Lou Adler". I added that he and I didn't need to go to New York and wait in the CBS-Fox office lobby to be called into a meeting with people in suits we didn't know.

I reminded him that we recently went to Fox Studios to see Studio Chairman Joe Roth, to kick off the studio's involvement in the 15th anniversary gala that would be hosted by them at the Fox Studio. Roth was his friend who had produced "Ladies and Gentlemen: The Fabulous Stains" (1982) that Lou directed. A security officer in a golf cart met us at the front gate and escorted Lou to a private parking space just feet from Roth's office. That kind of showtime and attention would not be available in a faceless New York office full of suited strangers.

There was really no reason at all to do anything but sit there in Malibu and wait for the CBS-Fox Video executives to show up. Let them come to the hilltop, which, of course, they did. Sitting in place, and controlling the energy, was more appropriate for Lou, who is a guy that is hypersensitive about his carefully curated mystique of his image. It really surprised me that he would want to come out from behind the protective screen that he so carefully nurtures and make that trip. The impulse to go to New York with hat in hand was the only time I had ever seen Lou lose his carefully cultivated mojo.

The 15th Anniversary party would wind up not only an amazing event celebrated by the fans but was going to be the biggest birthday bash for "Rocky Horror", a movie now well established in pop culture. The party not only packed sound stage 14 at Fox Studios, but was an important turning point in the movie's history.

A number of events were combined in the 15th Anniversary in 1990. They included:

May 1990 - The 4-album RHPS 15th Anniversary Box Set is released on CD and cassette.

Jul 1990 - Sal Piro's book about the RHPS experience, "Creatures of the Night", was published.

Oct 18, 1990 - The City of Los Angeles declared it "Rocky Horror Picture Show Day".

Oct 20, 1990 - RHPS celebrated its 15th Anniversary on Soundstage 14 at 20th Century Fox Studios, Century City, CA. Tim Curry, Richard O'Brien, Patricia Quinn, Little Nell, Barry Bostwick, and Meatloaf are in attendance. The event also marked the first appearance of a newly-mixed stereo track of the film, using masters from the soundtrack album.

Nov 8, 1990 - RHPS was released on VHS for the first time. The video included a stereo track, documentary footage, and a Time Warp video. A laserdisc was released later that year without the documentary. The RHPS Official Fan Club had started its own website.

Becca Walsh, an Austin, Texas fan for many years, who became a second-generation fan (after her dad) in the 21st century, reflected on the practicality of the home video when she said: "The video provides an opportunity when a midnight show is not locally available, especially if kids that want to see it are too young to go out to the theater at midnight." (5). The movie was "R" rated and inaccessible to young teenagers except on home video.

For Walsh, there was also a security blanket in having the video and DVD available now that Disney has absorbed Twentieth Century-Fox. "What if Disney were to say it's over? While Disney wants to portray an all-American image.....it will not cost them anything to have this…the fans are driving it; there are no costs to Disney. Yes there would be an outcry, but most of the fans would say we'll have our own clandestine showing, doing things our own way. We'd do the "Time Warp" in the backyard. Why not?" (6)

Fan Club President Sal Piro told me, "The fans have supported "Rocky Horror" for 45 years (in 2021). Who says they will not be there for as long as "Rocky Horror" lives?" (7)

Notes:

1. Pazuzu to author 3/6/21

2. O'Connor to author 1/20/21

3. https://time.com/3657605/fantasticks-history/

4. https://www.nytimes.com/2019/01/05/opinion/alexandria-ocasio-cortez-tax-policy-dance.html

5. interview with author 11/1/19

6. ibid

7. to author 5/23/19

Chapter 15
Merch Madness

The Industrialization of "The Rocky Horror Picture Show"

"There was no 'Rocky Horror' merchandise in the beginning. Just a promo t-shirt. People were making their own stuff to fit the demand for merchandise. I was a teenage girl working minimum wage at a coffee shop and I made my own buttons and t-shirts and sold them on the sidewalk at the Tiffany Theatre on the Sunset Strip to fans waiting to go into the midnight show. It was a crazy party environment. People were selling 'Rocky Horror' rice and other homemade merch. That was in the late 70's, people were just having fun hanging out outside the theatre. There was a 'Rocky Horror' sidewalk scene." This is how Lisa Sutton recalled the very early scene where fans, hungry for "Rocky Horror" memorabilia, filled the void by creating their own homemade souvenirs and trading or selling them to each other. (1)

The cottage industry of creating "Rocky Horror" merchandise slowly began to become professionalized, according to fan club president Sal Piro, who recounts that "At first there was a limited amount of merch...the soundtrack was the first thing in demand...but buttons, t-shirts,a book, posters, and magazines would follow". (2)

The large-scale merchandising of movie memorabilia by Fox was in its infancy when "Rocky Horror" started playing at midnight. "'The Planet of the Apes" (1968) movie had spun off a television series at Fox, and there was a modest merchandising effort for that" according to Rand Marlis, a young executive who was with the Fox merchandising program practically from the ground up as Director of Licensing at Fox. (3) "Apes" was "an American science fiction media franchise consisting of films, books, television series, comics, and other media."

"Today, the gross value of movie merchandising is $122 billion dollars", said Marlis, who, for over 30 years has been the owner of Creative Licensing Corporation, one of the industry's foremost independent merchandise licensing agencies. (4) Rand recalled that "Rocky Horror" was one of the earliest Fox films, outside of "Star Wars" to have significant licensed merchandise. (5)

Typically, a movie with music had a soundtrack album, and the one for "Rocky Horror" was released by Lou Adler's Ode label on September 25, 1975, the day before "The Rocky Horror Picture Show" had its US premiere at the UA Westwood Theater. An original cast recording from The Roxy had been released in 1974.

The first big, non-soundtrack merchandising effort by Fox for "The Rocky Horror Picture Show" was "The Rocky Horror Picture Show Book" by Bill Henkin", originally published in August 1979, a few years after the first midnight show at the Waverly.

Then, the floodgates opened. Rand Marlis assembled an array of merchandising tie-ins for the movie. "If you go online and find legitimate merchandise for "Rocky Horror" dating before 1983, when I left Fox to start Creative Licensing Corporation, I undoubtedly licensed it", he said (6) "Merchandising can be a lucrative part of a movie's revenue stream. "There are no typical splits between studios and producers in licensing. It depends on many factors, who is putting up the money, who are the other profit participants, what is the rest of the deal between the studio and the producer, etc. I can tell you that studios or licensing agencies normally get a commission of 25-35% off the top" said Marlis (7)

The decades of midnight show profits have been supplemented by growing profits from what would become a wide range of

200

merchandising. Hundreds of "for sale" items have worn the famous "Rocky Horror" lips.

Closely and emotionally connecting fans with their favorite movie or sports team is one of the important elements of the brand extension that comes with merchandising. Sports teams and some movie franchises like "Star Wars" have lifelong, multi-generational fans. So does "The Rocky Horror Picture Show".

In "Old Hollywood", stars had fan clubs that were generally created and maintained by the studios to keep their under-contract stars in the public view. As television soap operas became popular, fan clubs for them started to appear. But, movies and movie characters, with the notable exception of Disney, had not yet experienced the luster and profits that a well-run merchandising operation could bring. "The Rocky Horror Picture Show" has both: a well run fan club and a strong merchandising program.

Two of the biggest segments of fandom merchandising today, entertainment and sports, were valued at $150 billion annually in a 2019 report. Combined, they accounted for 53% of all merchandising in the year reported, with entertainment merchandising grossing $123 billion dollars and sports $28 billion of that total. (8) This highlights how important merchandising is not only as an additional revenue stream but in keeping a fan base solidly connected with "collectibles" from their favorite team or movie.

George Lucas understood this long before it dawned on Fox and potential merchandisers for "Star Wars" that characters, and other "Star Wars" licensing, would become a goldmine. Eventually, Disney would buy Lucasfilms and "Star Wars" from Lucas for four-billion-dollars (9) and add "Star Wars" collectibles and memorabilia to Disney's $57 billion merchandising empire. (10)

It wasn't all that easy for Fox in the beginning. While Lucas may have had a vision of what merchandising could do for him, potential licensees showed no interest. Marc Pevers recalls that, "As Vice President of Fox Licensing, I was responsible for the licensing campaign for the initial theatrical release of "Star Wars". Foolishly, few toy companies expressed any interest and many did not even bother to attend our presentations…to the toy industry in New York during February 1977."

"As detailed in the original production-distribution agreement between 20th Century Fox and Lucas, Fox administered the merchandising rights to 'Star Wars'. Lucas did have the right to approve all licensing deals. When the sequel rights were renegotiated, Fox relinquished the licensing rights to Lucas in 1979."

"We concluded what ultimately became a precedent shattering master toy license with Kenner Products Co. I negotiated this license, which remained in effect throughout the first two 'Star Wars' sequels." (11)

George Lucas ended up with both the sequels, and later the merchandising rights, to "Star Wars". Asked why Fox granted Lucas the merchandising rights, which were to add to the foundation of Lucas' billion dollar empire, his attorney Tom Pollack said Fox "wanted the sequel". (12)

As Pollack recounts it, "Jeff Berg, who was George's agent, took the treatment to Alan Ladd, Jr. at Fox, and Laddie said yes, I'll make this, and they negotiated the outline of the deal. George got $50,000 to write, another $50,000 to produce, and $50,000 to direct.

So, in the negotiations that were going on, we drew up a contract with Fox's head of business affairs, Bill Immerman, and me. We came to an agreement that George would retain the sequel rights.

Not all the rest of the stuff that came later, mind you, just the sequel rights. And Fox would get a first opportunity and last refusal right to make the movie.

In that deal for "The Empire Strikes Back" (1980), George made the decision to self-finance the film. Lucasfilm made a lot of money on "Star Wars" and would reinvest the money in the movie. The deal that was offered to Fox was you get distribution rights theatrically and video around the world for seven years, and we retain everything else. And, by the way, we want the merchandising back. Fox had started with the merchandising in that first year or two and did very well too. He wanted the merchandising back as of the time "Empire" came out. That meant soundtrack albums, music publishing, television, all rights other than the rights we were granting to Fox under this deal." (13)

I was showing Fox Chairman Barry Diller, a notoriously hard executive, the advertising campaign for an upcoming release one day when his assistant buzzed in to say that George Lucas was returning Diller's call. Diller was brief, saying, "George, I'd like to meet you whenever and wherever you want. It won't be onerous". I asked Diller what was up, and he said Fox was always at Lucas' disposal (not vice versa as would be normal), and the studio needed some concessions from George, who was known by then to be a director who never gave in to a studio.

Fox may have needed Lucas, but it was the other way around with "Rocky Horror"... Lou Adler needed Fox not only to keep the midnight movie machine minting out profits but to try replicating the midnight show experience outside of the United States and tie in a domestic merchandising program of soundtracks, boxed sets, books, and and miscellaneous "Rocky Horror" memorabilia.

While it may not reach the level of merchandising success as a professional sports team or "Star Wars", "The Rocky Horror Picture Show" is competitive when it comes to movie merchandise when you consider its music as merchandise. "Merch," the colloquialism for "merchandise," grew organically from the scrappy DIY memorabilia created by-fans-for-fans into a wide-ranging collection of items with wide-ranging appeal.

The growth of "merch," now a vast domestic merchandising operation, has exploded and has exploited "The Rocky Horror Picture Show" from records, fan books, remixes of the soundtrack, DVDs with commentaries, fan conventions, and prequels and remake movies. It may have become vulnerable when Disney acquired 20th Century Fox.

"All RHPS merch at the present time is by license with Disney and approved by us", says Adler (14)

What helps "Rocky Horror" merchandising is that it's active every day, it's not seasonal, and not tied to one movie as much as being tied to a seemingly never ending pop culture phenomenon.

Officially licensed merchandise, prior to the ARG deal, included dozens of individual items in predictable categories and popularly priced for fans. (15) The most significant single merchandising category has been music. When the movie soundtrack became linked to the success of the midnight show it turned into a second success story for the once-dead movie. Prior to the movie going midnight, Adler had released an original cast recording from the stage play at The Roxy, the very first attempt to find success with the music. Between 1974 and 2020, there have been eighteen "Rocky Horror" soundtrack albums released by Adler's Ode Records. (16)

There are also several dozen "Rocky Horror" derivative musical products that include 68 albums, with 94 recordings on109 pressings. Six box sets are also included. These albums include 1,159 tracks, of which 330 have song lyrics available, and 330 have MP3 sound files. A total of 13,255 tags have been applied using 669 distinct media tags, as well as 52 song tags and 12 language tags. (17)

Christy Walsh is credited as being the original sports agent in the modern era; he was Babe Ruth's agent. He used his automobile advertising and public relations training to create what Louis Menand calls the "Entertainment-media-merchandising combine that supplies much of the content for contemporary American culture".

"Walsh understood how that synergy worked, how the entertainment feeds the media and how the media feeds the sales." Menand continues "this multiplier effect is why the stars' incomes keep rising exponentially—why Tiger Woods, who has made about a hundred and twenty million dollars in prize money, is said to be worth close to a billion".

"Everyone," he said "in the (entertainment media merchandising) combine wants 'Tiger' to continue to make money, so they can continue to make money off Tiger". (18)

With "Rocky Horror", the movie is like Tiger, and the "combine" is Lou Adler and others that share in the profits. The "multiplier effect" is the reputation of the midnight phenomenon.

Taken together, they create what noted PR expert Jim McCarthy calls a "hothouse". He neatly summarizes the causes and effects of good marketing and merchandising when he says "I can't help thinking about how that broader marketing resonance often unfolds and grows in ways that aren't anticipated — like a hothouse effect.

I think the public has a general misconception that marketing is just something that is foisted on the public like a sort of soft hypnotism. But that's not what happens at all. In many ways, the public has an intuitive, engaged sense of what they prefer and the best marketers are the ones that can connect on that level." (19)

Adler personifies and personalizes the process. He credits his intuition to give the fans what they want when he says "Like everything else with 'The Rocky Horror Picture Show', it has been fan and fan club initiated and driven. The call-backs, the merch, the scratchy release prints..mono sound...I learned how to ride the wave and tried to assist...to improve and expand the elements as I felt they were asking for it". (20)

The best marketers and merchandisers for "Rocky Horror" are the community of fans themselves who operate in a type of multi-facet marketing and merchandising environment. Their outlets were the midnight shows where they participated in the "Rocky Horror" experience, the internet that is full of user groups and fan sites, and ultimately, the successful fan conventions.

In the fifty years of the midnight show, there have been eighty-nine fan events ranging from conventions (69), frequently recurring events (5), mini-conventions (4), and special events (89). (21)

Of all the merchandise and artifacts relating to and featuring "The Rocky Horror Picture Show" books, records, and dozens of other categories of licensed and branded materials, the Holy Grail for collectors is nothing that was ever officially released or sold.

For the 10th Anniversary, artist Charlie White was commissioned by Lou Adler to create a "Happy Birthday" poster. Charlie designed a tiered wedding cake, and on each tier, he placed miniature Japanese figurines that he turned into characters from "Rocky Horror". The first look at it was when a copy of the printed poster was delivered to the studio. "The studio was not involved until finished art...we worked with Charlie". (22)

The Fox legal department got cold feet when they saw the poster and worried that the figures were too reminiscent of Barbie Dolls which would be a copyright infringement of Mattel Toys, and ordered the posters destroyed. But, a small shipment of them had already been sent from the printer to New York to use at the Beacon Theater, site of the 10th Anniversary Celebration. They never got put up. In fact, whatever happened to them has been an enduring "Rocky Horror" mystery to this day.

How "The Rocky Horror Picture Show" will fit into the Disney family and Disney's $57 billion merchandising empire is another mystery. And, like all good mysteries, there may be some surprises.

Notes:

1. to author 8/12/19

2. interview with author Nov 26, 2019

3. interview with author January 23, 2020

4. ibid

5. interview with author August 12, 2019

6. interview with author April 24, 2020

7. ibid

8. https://licensinginternational.org/news/global-sales-of-licensed-products-and-services-reach-us-280-3-billion-fifth-straight-year-of-growth-for-the-licensing-industry/

9. https://thewaltdisneycompany.com/disney-to-acquire-lucasfilm-ltd/

10. https://www.cnbc.com/2017/04/18/star-wars-helps-make-disney-57-billion-in-licensed-products.html

11. https://www.latimes.com/archives/la-xpm-1999-jan-31-ca-3299-story.html

12. https://deadline.com/2015/12/star-wars-franchise-george-lucas-historic-rights-deal-tom-pollock-1201669419/

13. ibid

14. to author 1/9/21

15. http://www.rockyhorrorwiki.org/wiki2/index.php?title=Officially_Licensed_Merchandise_for_%27%27The_Rocky_Horror_Picture_Show%27%27

16. (http://www.rockyhorrorwiki.org/wiki2/index.php?title=Ode_Records

17. http://www.rockymusic.org/albums.php

18. "How Babe Ruth and Lou Gehrig Brought Stardom to the American Pastime" by Louis Menand, The New Yorker Magazine, pp 54-59, June 1, 2020

19. to author 6/2/20

20. to author 4/30/20

21. http://www.rockyhorrorwiki.org/wiki2/index.php?title=List_of_Conventions

22. to author 4/18/20

Chapter 16
Archer: The Lou Adler Legacy

What Lou Adler has left behind.

Lou Adler has a piano in his office and a collection of gold and platinum records and awards, tokens of his stature in the music business. He's also got several movies to his credit. Very few others in the music business can say this, although David Geffen comes to mind because he and Adler each had a pair of record labels: Geffen's Asylum Records and Geffen Records, while Adler had Dunhill Records and Ode Records. Geffen was also the "G" in DreamWorks SKG, the movie production company that he started in 1994 with Steven Spielberg and Jeffrey Katzenberg.

Both Adler and Geffen are examples of trying to convert success in one highly creative and competitive business (music) into another equally demanding and challenging business (movies).

Other than their notable Malibu beachfront mansions, their public differences are stark: Geffen is a very extroverted personality and a public philanthropist with his name on buildings, while Adler is introverted with practically no public persona other than sitting next to Jack Nicholson at Lakers basketball games.

Lou's philanthropy is producing annual fundraising events for The Painted Turtle, a West Coast Hole in the Wall Gang camp experience for children with serious medical conditions, that he started with his wife Page and Paul Newman in 1999. (1)

With his Monterey Pop Festival co-producer John Phillips, the modest Monterey International Pop Festival Foundation was created after the 1967 Festival to award low-scale grants to qualified organizations and individuals with identifiable needs in "music-related personal development, creativity, and mental and physical health." (2) Musicares, the thirty million dollar record industry charity with a similar mission established in 1989 by the National Academy of Recording Arts and Sciences, may have been inspired by it.

Highlights from Lou's discography and filmography reflect the influence of Sagittarius on his December 13 natal birth chart. The Sagittarian glyph is a quiver full of arrows, allowing the archer to shoot at multiple targets to increase the odds of a direct hit on one of them. His music archery was more successful than it was for his movies, as the following glossary of Lou's works shows.

Sam Cooke (1958)

While maybe he "don't know much about geography, don't know much trigonometry, don't know much about algebra, don't know what a slide rule is for" (3) Lou Adler does know how to generate success. This lyric, penned in 1958 when Lou was 25 years old, was the start of creating a key element of Lou's treasury: a copyright interest and/or music publishing rights for a creative work. Music publishing, an invisible and non-glamorous part of the music business, can be a goldmine for copyright holders who get a small royalty every time the music is played.

Music publishing is not where you make your reputation; it's where you make your money. The movie studio analog is their film library from which they can license titles forever.

Lou most likely learned this lesson in his very early days as the "West Coast song-plugger" for Don Kirshner's New York City-based music publishing company Aldon Music. (4)

The never-ending playing of "California Dreaming", a signature tune in Adler's legacy, could be the Golden State's anthem. It could also be a diagnosis for a feeling of bliss. It's so obviously a sentiment and lifestyle and was a cornerstone of Dunhill Records, a short-lived (1964-67) label started by Lou and a few others and fronted by Lou. Its first blockbuster group success was The Mamas and Papas, which added to the foundation of Lou's "sunshine pop" identification. But first, there was Jan and Dean.

Jan and Dean (1959)

In the fifties and early sixties, in the post-World War II expansion of a booming economy and good living, there was no place like California in the minds of many. It's where trends started that, a year or two later, would be hitting the rest of America.

The pristine California coastline, with its beautiful beaches, surfers, and "beach bunnies," was an iconic image and touchstone of the California Dream. Living "at the beach", preferably "on the beach", was seen as a capstone of success. Hula hoops and, in music, the "California sound" of laid-back music, and the car and hot rod scene were primary examples of "California culture," along with indoor/outdoor living, the BBQ, and a tolerant lifestyle that allowed anyone to be anything they wanted. Southern California was the apex of "California."

Music included such seminal examples as the Beach Boys, the Byrds, the Mammas and the Papas, and the Doors. Decades later, in tenser times, these sounds may have become nostalgic music but, in their infancy they were cutting edge anthems defining an aspirational lifestyle: everyone wanted to be "California Dreaming".

It would be a few more years before surf met psychedelia; Adler's 1967 Monterey Pop Festival would be an important midwife in synthesizing those two genres at one performance space in a groundbreaking festival. For now, there was purity and innocence and "sunshine pop" music, something Lou had an informal reputation for being "the father of".

It was not only California kids, but also their counterparts across the country that were listening to music about their lifestyle. The "California sound" became mythological. It was an era that Lou described as "Jan & Dean...surf music and culture, with the tall blond California look as opposed to Philadelphia Italian Frankie Avalon, Bobby Rydell, Fabian". (5)

Lou grew up in the East LA community of Boyle Heights, thirty-five miles away from his ultimate homestead of Malibu; it's a socio-economic distance the size of a major canyon. Lou had already been beach-initiated with Jan and Dean, a group he and Herb Alpert worked with and, in 1959, produced "Baby Talk" (1959), the first of a string of hits for the "California sound" duo. (6)

Jan and Dean preceded the Beach Boys.The Southern Californians mixed metaphors with songs like "Surf City" and "The Little Old Lady From Pasadena", highlighting the two most popular cultures of the era: surfing and cars.

As high-schoolers, Jan and Dean had collaborated on music, using different names and formats, but when Lou Adler and Herb Alpert worked with the newly named "Jan and Dean", their fortunes soared. Jan and Dean's "Baby Talk", when it charted at number 10, was another step for Lou into the hit music world. He had dipped his toe into the business with Sam Cooke, got in a little deeper with Jan and Dean, and eventually had one of the biggest footprints of the time in the business, and ultimately earned a place in the Rock and Roll Hall of Fame.

Baby Talk spent 12 weeks on the Billboard Hot 100 chart, peaking at No. 10, while reaching No. 28 on Billboard's Hot R&B Sides. (7) It was Lou's second time with a hit on the Billboard charts. His first was Sam Cooke's "Wonderful World", written and recorded in 1958 and released in 1961, which peaked at number 12 on the Billboard Hot 100 and hit number two on Billboard's Hot R&B Sides chart. (8) Lou's third trip to the charts would be with "California Dreaming" of the Mamas and Papas, and he would later dominate the charts with the ballads of Carole King.

Dunhill Records (1964)

Dunhill Records, started in 1964 by Adler, Bobby Roberts, Hal Landers, Jay Lasker, and Pierre Cossette, struck gold quickly with The Mamas and the Papas. (9) If Sam Cooke and Jan and Dean were significant artists for Lou Adler who were traveling along single lanes in Lou's road trip into music history, dealing with The Mamas and the Papas may have been the equivalent of traveling on the 405 freeway, the California interstate freeway that runs north-south through Los Angeles and is 14 lanes wide in some parts.

Adler had, in the Mamas and the Papas, what became a mid-60s supergroup that dominated in the years 1966 through 1968 when they released four hit albums that contained several top chart singles.

Papa John Phillips and his wife Michelle collaborated (he wrote, they both sang) with Mama Cass Elliott and Denny Doherty to form the high temple of California laid-back sound, with such tunes as "California Dreaming'", "Monday, Monday", "I Saw Her Again", "Dedicated To The One I Love", and "Twelve Thirty (Young Girls Are Coming To The Canyon)".

Guiding them, producing the sounds and songs that would make millions of fans and many millions of dollars, was Adler, who had a big challenge: how to get as much as possible out of this phenomenal group that was in a music world that was rapidly being revolutionized. The popular folk music idiom had burst into a new dimension in 1965, activated by Bob Dylan, one of the leaders of the American folk music revival, who went "electric" (and was

213

famously booed heavily for it by the audience) at the 1965 Newport Jazz Festival.

In just two years after Dylan's game-changing breakthrough, Lou would be placing the mellow, chorale-like Mamas and Papas on the Monterey Pop Festival stage back to back on Sunday (closing) night with the acid rock sounds of Janis Joplin and with Jimi Hendrix, a new artist that would add to the music revolution by burning his guitar on stage after playing a tune.

The arc from folk to fire was so short, just a couple of years, as musical tastes were quickly shifting. Adler sold Dunhill and the Mamas and the Papas to ABC at the height of their popularity.

Throughout his career, Lou appears to have been one step ahead of his contemporaries in predicting the pubic taste and capitalizing on it before moving on, reaching into his quiver for more arrows to loft. Maximizing while the group was hot and possibly seeing the darkness ahead, as Dylan sang "the times they are a changin'", that would become evident with the mid-sixties social and political turmoil.

Lou may have encouraged the Mamas and the Papas into producing the four albums in such a short span of time ('66 to '68), and then relentlessly following a pattern of releasing singles until the songs were well established before releasing an album. Of the seventeen singles released in this short period, six made the Billboard Top Ten. That's batting nearly 300, an average that would qualify the holder for entry into the Baseball Hall of Fame.

The Mamas and The Papas defined Lou Adler to a much larger audience. Many producers would be happy with this level of success, but the driven Adler was not one to give up, and he launched right into his next production, shifting from music man to impresario. With his Mamas and Papas colleague John Phillips, Lou

214

staged the 1967 Monterey International Pop Festival that would cleave his sunshine sounds into psychedelia. The counterculture was bifurcating into the soft and sunny sounds of Southern California that Lou was a tastemaker for and the darker, edgier music from San Francisco, as the pop festival would show.

Monterey International Pop Festival (1967)

Dunhill, the home of The Mamas and the Papas, was sold by Lou to ABC Records in 1967, the year he shifted gears from music producer to festival producer with the landmark Monterey International Pop Festival that he also used as a platform to make his first movie "Monterey Pop" (1968). Movie making was suddenly Lou's new creative outlet, running parallel to music making. It would be his "B-roll". In the next several years, Lou would attempt to become a rare creative hyphenate: a record producer and a movie producer. The various movie results would be disproportionate to the music results.

While Woodstock (1969) may have captured the headlines and become the media darling of outdoor rock festivals in the sixties, it was the Monterey International Pop Festival (June 16-18, 1967), produced by Lou Adler and John Phillips, that got there first, set the tone and introduced the new San Francisco sounds to the festival audience in a springboard that would capture the imagination of millions of hungry young people, who were consuming the new sounds with an energy as if they had been starved.

My playlist for the summer of '67, and at college that fall, included some of the new sounds that had been showcased at the Monterey Pop Festival, especially Big Brother and the Holding Company (Janis Joplin), Jefferson Airplane (Grace Slick) and The Jimi Hendrix Experience. Providing counterpoint were the more mellow sounds of The Byrds, Buffalo Springfield, Laura Nero, Otis Redding, and the Mamas and the Papas.

As events played out over the next couple of years, when Woodstock (August 15-18, 1969) and Altamont (December 6, 1969) happened, Monterey Pop would be called "A Cultural Highlight of the Sixties" by California media like the Santa Cruz Sentinel. (10) It helped build Adler's place in music history as an innovator, expanding his reach into audiences that went beyond a reliance on radio station programmers and the rumored payola necessary to get songs played. He was going over the head of the radio and to the audience directly, making a concert film of the event.

Lou got valuable experience in how to present music on a stage to a live audience, a skill that he honed with his music club, The Roxy, a few years later. The epitome of his stage musical experience would be "The Rocky Horror Show," which he presented at The Roxy before making the filmed version of it.

Woodstock (August 1969) was kids grooving in the rain and mud and enjoying themselves. The Altamont Speedway Free Festival (December 6, 1969) in Northern California was so fraught and tragic that the Grateful Dead, who had helped organize the event, declined to perform. Violence, heavy drugs, and death were elements of that disaster. In just two years, the spirit of Monterey Pop and the Summer of Love had morphed into darkness.

Lou Adler's characterization of the three big outdoor rock and roll festivals of the sixties was "At Woodstock, people remember the weather. At Altamont, remembered the murder. For Monterey Pop, people remember the music" (11)

The Monterey Pop Festival also marked a turning point in the dominance of sunny, happy, upbeat music; the trends mirroring society at the time were going the other way, toward an eve of destruction that, in the morning light, would see the political assassinations of Robert F. Kennedy and Martin Luther King, Jr., the deaths of musicians (often from drug-related overdoses), the anti-Vietnam War movement, one US President (Johnson) being forced to abandon hopes for a second term, while his successor (Nixon) was forced from office for near-criminal acts. Underlying and deeply affected by all of this was the explosion of a counterculture of turned-on-tuned-in kids who did not want the status quo in music ,politics, movies, or life to continue.

The Monterey Pop Festival was the perfect bridge between the safe present and the uncertain future, although the seismic change in tastes did not affect Adler. He was yet to enjoy his biggest musical success a few years later with the soft and tender ballads of Carole King—something as far away from the San Francisco sound as he could be. Where "peace and love" had fizzled—the hippie-branded "summer of love" became more of a slogan than a lifestyle—Adler and his taste for pure romance flourished, as evidenced by his work with singer and songwriter King.

The cultural environment that surrounded Lou in the mid-60s was brand new to everyone. Disaffected youth, who had legitimate claims against almost anything the establishment was doing, were becoming outspoken in their attempts to claim a voice in what their future would be. The hippie movement, that was anti-Vietnam War and promoted peace and love instead, was percolating and would explode in San Francisco, with Haight-Ashbury (the neighborhood intersected by those two streets) as ground zero for hippies.

As more and more disaffected counterculture youth migrated to San Francisco, the feeling that 1967 could be "The Summer of Love" was growing into a promising lifestyle. This made some people happy and others wary. "Peace and love" sounded too good to be true. Sure enough, that experiment lasted less than nine months, in what historians bracketed by two seminal events: the "Human Be-In Rally" in San Francisco on January 14, 1967, and a mock funeral, the "Death of the Hippie" ceremony on October 6, 1967.

This was the background for the Monterey International Pop Festival, held at the Monterey County Fairgrounds on the weekend of June 16, 1967, one week after I had walked into MGM, where I would become a teenage intern for Stanley Kubrick on "2001: A Space Odyssey". It was only a couple of years later that I took "Rocky Horror" to midnight.

Nobody had attempted an outdoor, three days and nights rock and roll festival like this before. The very famous Newport Jazz Festival was a reference point, but its audiences were polite and cultured. Unpredictable was what a swarming of hippies descending on the Monterey Peninsula would be like. The popular image was counterculture, anti-establishment, anti-Vietnam War, sex, drugs, and rock and roll. San Francisco was the leading edge of acting out by America's youth.

Lou Adler was a skilled promoter and found a way to soften the anxieties about hippies and the counterculture youth lifestyle that was one without some of the normal boundaries of society. He did it through song, in a tune that was a counterpoint to the hard edge sounds coming from San Francisco; those sounds were becoming a magnet for the growing underground alternative youth culture that was rejecting mainstream America, turning instead to the San Francisco sounds and psychedelic lifestyle.

John Phillips got together with Scott McKenzie and wrote a tune called "San Francisco, Be Sure to Wear Flowers in Your Hair", a syrupy chamber of commerce type song. McKenzie sang it, and Adler produced and promoted it for his new Ode Records label. The

218

art for the record featured a picture of the non-threatening, boy-next-door-looking McKenzie. The song was very subtle propaganda that glorified the counterculture, taking away it's hard edges and uncertainties. It laid out the premise of *"All across the nation, such a strange vibration, people in motion, there's a whole generation, with a new explanation"* and then offered the solution promising "gentle people" a summertime "love-in," and people "with flowers in their hair." The song helped to promote the Festival but also offered a softer look at what was being called "the summer of love" in San Francisco, with the song's refrain of:

"If you're going to San Francisco

You're gonna meet some gentle people there

For those who come to San Francisco

Summertime will be a love-in there

In the streets of San Francisco

Gentle people with flowers in their hair."

(12)

Observed Clive Davis, the head of Columbia Records, which was the distributor of Lou's new Ode Records label after Lou sold Dunhill and the Mamas and The Papas to ABC, it was "not only a great song, but a brilliant marketing and promotion move.....that captured a cultural moment in a way that was made for AM radio, and it became a Top 5 hit." (13)

The acts that were assembled to perform at Monterey were a mix of the known and the new, with many of the latter categories representing what was being called the "San Francisco sound", that has been described by SF Gate as music that "worked best in a dance hall, under the influence of psychedelics with a liquid light show and an unreadable concert handbill to take home." (14)_ Radio,

219

except for the advent that summer of FM radio, was not prepared to showcase this sound that was not formatted into the three-minute single model that drove airplay. Best appreciated when jammed live and without many boundaries, only some courageous radio stations would play it.

Somehow that added to the appeal of it as underground music, to be experienced in person at a live show, in an act of communal bonding. That same dynamic—having to be there in person to get and share the experience—is what makes the midnight show of "The Rocky Horror Picture Show" so successful.

Like being in a light show surrounded by sounds, you have to be in a theater with the audience, and shadow cast participation to get the full experience of "Rocky Horror".

Some examples of the new sounds booked at Monterey included Jefferson Airplane (Grace Slick), Country Joe & the Fish, Big Brother and the Holding Company (Janis Joplin), the Grateful Dead, and The Jimi Hendrix Experience. Providing counterpoint were the more mellow sounds of Simon and Garfunkel, Johnny Rivers, The Byrds, Buffalo Springfield, Laura Nero, Otis Redding, and the Mamas and the Papas.

The closing night lineup defined the starkness of choice, the shadow and light chiaroscuro becoming available in music, with a reprise by Janis Joplin of her riveting breakthrough Saturday afternoon performance (the only act to play twice at the festival), and Jimi Hendrix lighting his guitar on fire during his stage performance, with a hard cut to the finale: the Mamas and the Papas, singing an almost dated soft and soothing night-time lullaby under the starry sky, to close out the festival. This hard and soft combination of sounds made history by showing the ebbing tide of the present, foreshadowed by the exciting waves of the future.

Watching the movie of the concert, sixty years later, is one of the best examples of how pop culture was changing rapidly.

Looking back at the cultural revolution that shortly followed it, the Thursday before the Friday opening of the Monterey Pop Festival may have been the end of an era, when the musician descendants of bobby-sox music turned inward and introspective, using themes of alienation, dissatisfaction, and resistance, and when soft sounds were replaced with hard-edged lyrics pushing a social and political movement driven by youth.

"Ultimately, the Monterey Pop Festival belonged to Hendrix. He arrived as a relative unknown to become the personification of organizer John Phillips' intentions for three days of inclusivity and adventure during the Summer of Love. It is a bitter irony that Phillips had scheduled his group, the Mamas and the Papas, to close the weekend – i.e. to go on right after Hendrix. Their gentle pop looked decidedly anachronistic: there could be no doubt that rock's baton had been passed forward." (15) .

Hendrix had not been sought after to perform at Monterey Pop. "Indeed, the Jimi Hendrix Experience only made it on to the bill after strong lobbying from Paul McCartney, a member of the festival's organizing committee". The future "Sir Paul - CH MBE" with his Beatles colleagues, had dominated the sixties soundscape, but his ear told him it was the sounds of Hendrix, and others like him, that people would be listening to as soft rock became the new nostalgia in a music world that was becoming saturated in psychedelia. (16)

It could have been a significant turning point for Lou Adler, moving from his familiar pretty ballads and surf sounds to keep up, or even try to be ahead of the coming tidal wave of social revolution expressed by contemporary musicians and their bands. But, he took a break from producing music and stepped into Hollywood instead, first producing a concert film of the Monterey Pop Festival (1968) and then producing Robert Altman's "Brewster McCloud" (1970). It would be nearly five years before Lou returned to the recording studio with Carole King, whose success set new standards.

Monterey Pop (1968)

"Monterey Pop" (1968), the movie, was shot by D.A. Pennebaker, who had just filmed a Bob Dylan documentary. He was commissioned by Adler to film the festival under an arrangement with ABC-TV that would showcase it as a movie of the week. The network had given Lou $200,000 as an advance. It would be his first attempt at filmmaking, and it eventually achieved some underground cult status despite a rejection by ABC-TV.

"We showed Tom Moore, the head of ABC at the time, and a very conservative Southern gentleman, Jimi Hendrix, fornicating with his amp and we said. "What do you think?" Adler recalls. And he said, "Keep the money and get out." He said, "Not on my network." (17)

A decade later, with "The Rocky Horror Picture Show", Lou would face another crossroads in pop culture, as significant as the changeover from soft to hard music, when he chose to embrace a nascent, underground LGBTQ+ audience for "The Rocky Horror Picture Show", an audience that he recognized long before many of his contemporaries ever acknowledged it. Like the disparagement of Hendrix by ABC, the CEO of Fox did not have kind words for "Rocky Horror", objecting to a marketing campaign that he called "lewd and lascivious" and demanding that the Fox name be removed from the campaign.

Ode Records (1968)

The sale of Dunhill Records and his diversion into producing a pop festival and a movie about that festival did not diminish Lou's place in the music world: he bounced back with a new label called Ode Records. It became home for many acts and the primary source for "The Rocky Horror Picture Show" music. Between 1974 and 2016, Ode released seventeen "Rocky Horror" albums, a considerable sleight of hand achievement considering that they all contain the same music. It's just the packaging and features that change. Lou excels at packaging, brand extensions, and ancillaries. His empire of albums is a dividend of the success of the midnight show. Before that, the album had been dropped by CBS for a lack of sales when the movie had been a box-office failure. (18)

Ode's new distribution deal with AM Records reunited Adler with his original writing and producing partner, Herb Alpert, and one of their first promotion men, Jerry Moss. Herb Alpert and Jerry Moss had all worked for Aldon Music early in their music careers. (19)

A "Rocky Horror" music fan has tracked "68 albums, with 94 recordings on 109 pressings. Six box sets are also included. There have also been forty-two CD's of the "Rocky Horror" music releases between 1973 to 2007." (20). That's a lot of music licensing and royalties. While Ode had been released by A&M, Lou now had his own "A and M" in the way of Ancillaries and Merch.

The turnaround of the movie into a midnight hit created new revenue streams not only for the movie but the music and the merch.

Brewster McCloud (1970)

Lou's first feature theatrical film attempt, "Brewster McCloud" (1970), started out as a probable "can't miss" and ended up mostly forgotten. It paired Monterey Pop Festival producer Lou Adler with emerging director Robert Altman, fresh off his success with "Mash" (1970) would be making his movie at Metro-Goldwyn-Mayer, one of the strongest studios of the day. Altman was experimenting with his layering of sound technique; the Houston Astrodome provided the filming location and publicity platform. But, MGM was suddenly under the control of new owner Kirk Kerkorian, a Las Vegas casino czar, who was telling his studio head Jim Aubrey to liquidate MGM. Lou and "Brewster McCloud" didn't stand a chance.

Carole King (1971)

Fortunately for Lou, he had a new label, Ode Records, and a new act, Carole King, to spend his creative energy on.

The year 1971, when Lou Adler next showed up in the pop culture scene in a big way, was an exciting and inspiring time, highlighted by great directors like Stanley Kubrick ("A Clockwork Orange"), Robert Altman ("McCabe and Mrs. Miller"), Hal Ashby ("Harold and Maude"), William Friedkin ("The French Connection"), Peter Bogdanovich ("The Last Picture Show"), Woody Allen ("Bananas"), and Bernardo Bertolucci ("The Last Tango In Paris"). Francis Ford Coppola was busy preparing "The Godfather" for release. These directors were making box office history in the movies in 1971. That same year, barely-out-of-school newcomers George Lucas and Steven Spielberg each made their first movies: "THX1138" and "Duel," respectively.

In music, disco was starting to take hold, featuring dance music for a new urban nightlife subculture that devoured it. A few years later, with "Saturday Night Fever" (1977), disco had become mainstream and a leading musical form. With EDM (electronic dance music), disco's expression has extended its life span in clubs, raves, and festivals to the present. It and rap are two mainstays of music today, but neither form had attracted Adler, just as the hard-edged psychedelia sounds he showcased at the Monterey Pop Festival did not rub off on his taste buds.

"Disco came in, [and] I wasn't interested in that," Adler told the Jewish Journal in a reflective interview four decades later in which he touched on some of his career and personal highlights. (21)

What did interest Lou was singer-songwriter Carole King, with whom he made records that set records and won Grammy awards, including Album of the Year, Record of the Year ("It's Too Late"), Song of the Year ("You've Got a Friend"), and Best Pop Vocal Performance-Female.

Of his many achievements in music, this collaboration capped his music career and sent him to the Rock and Roll Hall of Fame. It was also Lou's last pure play in producing music. After this, he would shift his time and creativity to his nightclub (The Roxy), a comedy act (Cheech and Chong), a handful of movies (including "The Rocky Horror Picture Show"), and what he has called "my greatest productions": his seven sons. (22) Nicholai, Cisco, Manny, Ike, Oscar, Pedro, and Sonny are genetically imbued to be music-men of their own definitions as they grow into their individual identities. He also has a daughter named Honey, who is Sonny's sibling.

The five years Carole King spent at Ode (1971-76) were Lou Adler's golden years. No single project, including the five decades of continuous midnight theatrical showings of "The Rocky Horror Picture Show", would displace Carole King as the endeavor most closely identified with the success of Lou Adler. Even the very popular comics Cheech and Chong, who were Lou's only crossover act as both record and movie projects, did not have the sustained mass appeal that King had, or the longevity with Lou.

Starting with "Tapestry", Carole King delivered six albums to Ode Records that charted at positions 1-1-2-6-1-3. One of them ("Tapestry" in 1971) set a record for how long it spent on the Billboard charts, 6 years second only to Pink Floyd's "The Dark Side of the Moon" which was released two years after "Tapestry" and spent 14 years on the charts.

Carole King's "new material on 1971's 'Tapestry' hit a chord with the world," music writing colleague Cynthia Weil said, explaining King's attraction. Weill added that "Carole spoke from her heart, and she happened to be in tune with the mass psyche. People were looking for a message, and she came to them with a message that was exactly what they were looking for." (23) While Pink Floyd was taking listeners on head trips, Carole King was touching hearts.

Lou Adler and Ode Records, his boutique label that emphasized quality over quantity, enjoyed a luster of extreme prosperity driven by King's delivery of hit after hit after hit.

Basketball Jones (1973)

Dipping into visuals, again after "Monterey Pop" (1968) and "Brewster McCloud" (1970), Lou produced a promo video called "Basketball Jones" (1973) to help build awareness for a Cheech and Chong album. It remains my favorite Lou Adler visual production. I did not like "The Rocky Horror Picture Show," but I loved "Basketball Jones", and I wished Lou had gone further down that direction of animation married to music. It's a format that fits perfectly for today and it could have been groundbreaking five decades ago to have him be an animation producer. He transferred the video to 33mm film stock, and we played it ahead of "Rocky Horror" at the UA Westwood when the movie opened a couple of years later.

The song is about teenage Tyrone and his love of basketball, sung in a falsetto voice by Cheech Marin and a backing band consisting of George Harrison, Klaus Voormann, Carole King, Nicky Hopkins (piano), Tom Scott (sax), Billy Preston (organ), Jimmy Karstein (drums) and Jim Keltner (percussion). Ronnie Spector, Michelle Phillips, and The Blossoms with Darlene Love were the backing cheerleaders' voices. "That was a wild session," Adler recalls. "I probably called Carole [King] and told her to come down, but with Harrison and [Klaus] Voorman—I didn't call and say come in and play. Everyone happened to be in the A&M studios at that particular time, doing different projects. It was spilling out of the studio into the corridors." (24)

The Roxy (1973)

"Let's make the best rock 'n' roll club that L.A. has seen, with the best sound and the best seating and treat everybody really good" declared Lou Adler when Whisky a Go Go and Rainbow co-owner Elmer Valentine said to him, "You know, we should open this club." (25) It would be a counterpoint to the Troubadour, which, according to Lou, "was the only game in town as far as rock 'n' roll. Even though it was folk-ish, they started playing a lot of rock 'n' roll artists, and they were very tough on the musicians. You had to sign a seven-time engagement contract — and the money never got very good." (26)

Lou, Elmer Valentine, and music figures David Geffen, Elliot Roberts, and Peter Asher opened the club on September 23, 1973, with Neil Young (his future brother-in-law; Young and Lou married Hannah sisters Daryl and Page) as the opening act.

For over fifty years, the Adler family has owned The Roxy, which has met that "best" standard and achieved iconic status as one of the Sunset Strip's most famous venues of its day.

227

The Roxy is best understood in context. It's at the epicenter of the fabled Sunset Strip, long a magic set of words that mean nightlife, rock and roll, and party.

The private eye TV series "77 Sunset Strip", popular in the 1960's, was my first awareness of the Sunset Strip. For Lou, the Strip was a destination and lifestyle far removed from his Boyle Heights home in East Los Angeles. "I probably started going to Sunset Boulevard when I was just out of the Navy, probably 20 years old", Adler told the LA Times in a nostalgic review of how meaningful the location is to him. (27)

The Roxy and "The Rocky Horror Show" had a symbiotic relationship; each benefitted from the other. The club needed live performance acts every night, and "The Rocky Horror Show" that Lou saw in London and wanted to bring to LA needed a stage.

A stage play, that would run longer than an act playing for a few nights, would help keep the club booked, and "Rocky Horror" would give Lou a dazzling draw that would help promote his new club. It was a fateful fit that grew into "The Rocky Horror Picture Show" movie. Six months after The Roxy opened, "The Rocky Horror Show" opened on March 21, 1974, and ran for several months before the cast left for England to film the movie.

Eventually, "The Rocky Horror Picture Show" would play very successful midnight shows at the Tiffany Theatre, a short walk down the Strip from The Roxy, adding "the Sunset Strip" to its legend.

The Rocky Horror Picture Show (1975)

So many factors entered into the failure and then the success of "The Rocky Horror Picture Show" that it would take a book to recount the studio experiences and the fan experiences that made it all happen. This volume is that book.

Forever (1977)

The one that got away, the movie I hoped Lou Adler would make, was "Forever", based on the 1935 Mildred Cram novella. It tells "the love story of Colin and Julie who meet before they were born and finally find each other again in life…a mystery of tenderness and fragility, and a love that was longer than life and stronger than death." (28)_ Lou may have been involved as a producer to help his friend director Hal Ashby, who was tentatively slated by MGM to make the movie in the spring of 1977 after Ashby's successful "Bound For Glory" (1976) that was nominated for an Academy Award for Best Picture. Describing "Forever", Ashby's biographer called "the fifty-eight page story of love and reincarnation…near impossible to adapt for the screen…Ashby pulled out of the deal." (29)

It's a story that has hit a nerve with readers since the day it was published nine decades ago. Legendary MGM production head and "boy wonder" Irving Thalberg had MGM purchase it as a vehicle for his wife, Norma Shearer. He died tragically at age 37 the next year, and the movie was not made.

Neither animation nor special effects were used to drive movies in the mid-70's, and one technique or the other may have helped make this movie. Stephen Spielberg had just made "Jaws" (1975), the precursor to the new wave of special effects movies that George Lucas hammered home with "Star Wars" (1977). The only movies using animation were the saccharine Disney offerings. Had the Spielberg-Lucas type of special effects come a few years earlier, or the production of "Forever" pushed back a couple of years, using them to interpret "Forever" may have made making the movie viable. But "Forever", a timeless love story, was ahead of its time.

Up In Smoke (1978)

Riding the Carole King tidal wave of success, Lou shifted from love ballads to the ethnic, drug-centric, street-smart comedy performed by Cheech and Chong, an act he discovered at the Troubadour. Several of their comedy albums, produced by Lou on Ode Records, were released in the next five years. Lou also produced and directed their first movie, "Up In Smoke" (1978).

This was the epitome for Lou as a record producer and movie maker on one project. It shared a few things with "Rocky Horror". Audiences for both were people on the margins of society: the gay and lesbian community ("Rocky Horror") and stoners ("Up In Smoke"). Both were crossover projects—the music and movie symbiosis worked for each as Hollywood often dreamed of but rarely accomplished. The movie soundtrack for one, and the comedy albums for the other.

The movie also gave Lou, often identified by his headgear, a new hat to wear: movie director. Producing a record can be a solitary job. It's just you, the musicians and the sound engineer. Movie directors interact with dozens of crew members each day, needing to sign off on just about every decision, no matter how big or small. "It's the difference between an engineer and a second versus a crew of over a hundred awaiting a decision and direction". (30) By the time the movie was filmed in May and June 1977, Cheech and Chong had enjoyed success with five comedy albums which would have been thought to be enough awareness of them to lure their audience into theaters. Paramount initially was for the movie, putting $1,000,000 into the production budget, but then cooled on it, causing Adler to invest an additional $800,000 that was needed to complete it. (31)

Studio president Michael Eisner saw a rough cut and wasn't impressed. Adler's response was to buy back the film from

Paramount. (32)_ Positive test screenings changed Eisner's mind, and Paramount released the movie, which became a huge box-office success.

Shock Treatment (1981)

Predictably, once was not enough. The hunger and temptation to capitalize on the success of "The Rocky Horror Picture Show" would answer a few questions ranging from could it be done, was it necessary, and what would the fans say? The answers came with the release of "Shock Treatment" (1981), five years after the launch of what would be a very successful midnight run of "Rocky Horror". It was written like "Rocky Horror" by Richard O'Brien and Jim Sharman, directed by Sharman, and produced by Lou Adler and Michael White; the team was identical to the "Rocky Horror Picture Show".

Lou arranged a screening for me at his Malibu office one Saturday morning, and we spoke right afterward. He must have sensed the disappointment in my face and my voice as I told him I didn't like it, but that did not deter him. After all, it's the same reply I gave him years earlier when he asked me how I liked "Rocky Horror". The difference this time was that, unlike "Rocky Horror", I didn't believe in "Shock Treatment".

Roger Ebert, a key film critic, hit the nail on the poseur's head when he said that he felt "Rocky Horror" fans would reject a movie that was specifically targeted at them, remarking that "cult film audiences want to feel that they have seen the genius of something that everybody else hates. They discovered this film, they know it's good, everyone else thinks it's garbage". (33)

The internet and global online fan community for "Rocky Horror" was years away, so fan reaction could only be demonstrated by their not accepting it at the box-office. Fox released the movie on Halloween as a midnight show and then shelved it.

The artifice of calling it "not a sequel, not a prequel, but an equal" fooled nobody. As a marketer, I would have called that a damaging claim that would be hard to deliver on, but I had left Fox by then.

Ladies and Gentlemen: The Fabulous Stains (1982)

"They didn't understand the movie...the distribution and marketing people didn't know what to do with it", (34) said Lou Adler, as if he were in an echo chamber having the same problem at Paramount with "Ladies and Gentlemen The Fabulous Stains" (1982) as he had five years earlier with "The Rocky Horror Picture Show" (1975) at Fox.

It was a movie I had a peripheral interest in after leaving Fox. Afternoons around the pool and BBQ evenings surrounded by family in the very quiet rural countryside, my summer vacation from my Fox studio job in 1979 was five weeks long and the perfect time and space to reflect on "what's next?". I read Barbara Tuchman's "The Proud Tower" about the lead up to World War I, and considered where I may be headed. Laddie (Alan Ladd Jr.) had just resigned from Fox where, as studio president, he had backed me and my midnight plan for "The Rocky Horror Picture Show". When I returned to the studio after Labor Day, I turned in my own resignation. Without Laddie, Fox would be just another movie studio trying to make it. His Periclean Age had brought seventeen Academy Award nominations or wins, and the team of us that he had assembled was known as one of the best in Hollywood. Without him running the studio, there was no point to remaining at Fox.

Two filmmakers knew what I was going to be contemplating over my August break: Lou Adler and Mel Brooks. I worked very closely with Mel on the marketing for his Fox movies: "Young

Frankenstein" (1974), "Silent Movie" (1976), and "High Anxiety" (1977), and with Lou on "The Rocky Horror Picture Show" (1975), which was now a huge midnight success, so I gave each a heads up that I was considering following Laddie out the door.

Mel gave me an accolade of "you know how to string the pearls" and a contract to become effective the day after I left Fox; he hired me to represent him for marketing on his next Fox movie ("Fatso"- 1980). Lou sent me a script called "All Washed Up" to my vacation location and asked me to read it. A story of an all-girl punk band's meteoric rise and fall, the movie would be renamed "Ladies and Gentlemen: The Fabulous Stains" (1982).

Eventually, I went to New York with Lou to meet with Frank Mancuso, President of Paramount, so Lou could pitch him on the "Stains" movie that Lou would direct and his friend Joe Roth would produce along with Lou.

Lou and Mancuso had just enjoyed huge success with "Up In Smoke" (1978) at Paramount, and the studio felt like the perfect fit for Lou. But, it wasn't. Just like the disappointment with "Brewster McCloud" (1970) at MGM several years earlier, this project looked good on paper, but not in reality. Joe Roth was a seasoned producer and aware of how to work with a studio distribution organization to benefit his movie. But, that didn't help.

Despite his recent "Up In Smoke" success at Paramount, the sales and marketing executive talent that shepherded that winner through the studio was apparently MIA for Lou on this movie.

Frank Mancuso, then a 20-year Paramount veteran who headed distribution when Lou had "Up in Smoke" at the studio and now had "The Fabulous Stains" to release, could have guaranteed executive buy-in of Lou's project.

This shows how internal controls, or lack of them, can make or break a movie; how fateful it can be to have one studio executive believing in your movie, who can run the inside-the-studio-walls ground game for it, like I did for "The Rocky Horror Picture Show". It's why personal relationships are so critical to Hollywood's success.

It's hard to understand that the Adler-Roth-Mancuso combo was unable to activate and excite the marketing and distribution staffs at Paramount. Roth, soon to be the studio head at Fox, and Mancuso, who would become Paramount's studio head right after the movie was released, could have created internal energy for "Stains".

Trying to untangle the eventual failure of the movie, Lou asked a question many people ask all the time about many movies: "Well, I think the real question is, why was it even made? I think Paramount did it for two reasons. One, the writer Nancy Dowd was an Academy Award winner for "Coming Home" (1978), and I'd just come off the success of directing "Up in Smoke (1978)". And those two elements — you can see the psyche of the studio, that says "let's make it!" even if they don't understand it or know how to market it. Once it was finished, they'd done their work; they didn't have to do anything to protect the jobs that had to be protected. So the film just lay there. They didn't do anything with it." (35)

While Lou may have never uttered the word "failure," it clearly was one, and Paramount's un-involvement was exacerbated by a years-long delay over how the movie would end that pitted the writer Nancy Dowd against the producer-director Adler. Those creative differences, not unusual in Hollywood, would have a silver lining. "The film wrapped in 1980 without an ending. Two years went by. The director came up with his own closing scene - a faux music video that recast The Stains as pop stars. That version tanked in test screenings and was never released. But within a few years, it started surfacing on late-night cable TV and then on bootlegs. Bratmobile's Allison Wolfe says many young women who saw those grainy VHS tapes not only became fans of The Stains but were inspired to form their own bands". (36)

Lou's coda to the "Stains" experience was, "That could be the reason I didn't go on directing". (37)

It would become Lou's fifth and final movie for a studio, although twenty-six years later, he would produce a television movie for the Fox television network called "The Rocky Horror Picture Show: Let's Do the Time Warp Again" (2016).

"The Rocky Horror Picture Show: Let's Do the Time Warp Again" (2016)

They are "all 'Rocky' fans!" (38) exclaimed Kenny Ortega when he described the cast of "The Rocky Horror Picture Show: Let's Do The Time Warp Again" (2016) television movie remake of the midnight show phenomenon he would be directing for producer Lou Adler and the Fox Television Network.

Conflating actors who are fans of a movie they are auditioning to hopefully be cast in, with fans of the movie because of the community it has built for them may have been the fatal first step to the idea that "The Rocky Horror Picture Show" could be "remade". The lesson of the failure of "Shock Treatment" (1981), billed as "not a sequel, not a prequel, but an equal," had already challenged producer hubris. Rejection by the fans was about to happen again.

Forty years after the first midnight show of "Rocky Horror," and three generations of fans later, an attempt was made to recapture magic through an alchemy of a devoted fan base and boldly casting a transgender African American in Tim Curry's iconic role.

"As you can imagine, when we announced we were doing this, there was tremendous backlash from fans," said executive producer Lou Adler. (39) The Latin phrase *cui bono?* (who benefits?) provided an answer. Adler was right, the fans had already spoken before the cameras rolled. It wasn't to be for their benefit at all.

Richard O'Brien's lyrics to the song "Let's Do The Time Warp Again" perfectly capture the dilemma of how to remake a cult classic: "With a bit of a mind flip, you're into the time slip, and nothing can ever be the same. You're spaced out on sensation like you're under sedation. Let's do the Time Warp again".

"Some things can't be replicated or recaptured, and thanks to Fox, we now know that one of them is the subversive magic of 'The Rocky Horror Picture Show'…The old saw about imitation being the sincerest form of flattery isn't really true for remakes — find something fresh, or go home — yet imitation is what mostly comes to mind here," said the critic from the New York Times. (40)

The best barometer of success is box-office, or, in the case of a television movie, the broadcast ratings. The numbers came in, and they were disappointing. "Fox-TV's special October 20 broadcast of "The Rocky Horror Picture Show: Let's Do the Time Warp Again" earned an average household overnight rating of 3.4/5 for the 8-10 PM time slot. The ratings for the TV movie were 54 percent below the network's January 31, 2016, live Broadway musical-style production, "Grease: Live", which drew a 7.4/11 average rating. Ratings also declined 26 percent from the first hour to the last. This showed that people did not stick with watching the movie. (41)

With very little fan investment in the remake and weak viewership, this became an asterisk in the "Rocky Horror" canon.

The Total Works

Lou Adler, music man, has an enviable collection of music hits, an induction into the Rock and Roll Hall of Fame, and a very successful Sunset Strip nightclub.

On the movie side of Lou's creative output ledger, "The Rocky Horror Picture Show", as a midnight show, has been a phenomenal success. "Up In Smoke", produced and directed by Lou, was a huge box-office hit. Cheech Marin and Tommy Chong used it to set themselves up for several more successful movies. The two attempts to spin-off "Rocky Horror" with "Shock Treatment" and "The Rocky Horror Picture Show: Let's Do the Time Warp Again" did not do so well, nor did "Ladies and Gentlemen: The Fabulous Stains". A studio's inability to properly support "Brewster McCloud" doomed it, and "Monterey Pop" has become a historical artifact. The very inspired "Basketball Jones" was merely a promo piece.

Lou Adler, the Sagittarius archer, has hit many of his targets, more in music than in movies, leaving a legacy of memorable mid-century pop culture moments that fairly represent a man and his time.

Notes:

1. https://jewishjournal.com/uncategorized/214558/lou-adler-low-key-lucky-and-very-cool/

2. https://montereyinternationalpopfestival.com/pages/foundation

3. Songwriters: Herb Alpert / Lou Adler / Sam Cooke - Wonderful World lyrics © Abkco Music, Inc.

4. https://www.britannica.com/topic/Lou-Adler-1688313

5. to author 4/20/19

6. Gilliland, John (1969). "Show 20 - Forty Miles of Bad Road: Some of the best from rock 'n' roll's dark ages. [Part 1]" (audio). Pop Chronicles. University of North Texas Libraries

7. https://en.wikipedia.org/wiki Baby_Talk_(Jan_and_Dean_song)#cite_note-3

8. https://en.wikipedia.org/wiki Wonderful_World_(Sam_Cooke_song)\

9. Pierre Cossette "Another Day In Show Business: One Producer's Journey" – ECW Press - 2002

10. https://www.santacruzsentinel.com/2017/06/14/the-1967-monterey-pop-festival-remains-the-cultural-high-point-of-the-sixties/

11. Lou Adler interview, p.199 in "The Hippies: A 1960s History", by John Anthony Moretta, McFarland & Co., Inc. Publishers, 2017

12. San Francisco-Be Sure to Wear Flowers in Your Hair. Songwriter: John Edmund Andrew Phillips © Universal Music Publishing Group

13. Clive Davis: The Soundtrack of My Life, pp. 61-63

14. https://www.theguardian.com/music/2020/aug/03/jimi-hendrix-monterey-pop-1967-a-live-performance-never-bettered

15. https://www.theguardian.com/music/2020/aug/03/jimi-hendrix-monterey-pop-1967-a-live-performance-never-bettered

16. ibid

17. https://www.npr.org/2017/06/15/532978213/a-look-back-at-monterey-pop-50-years-later

18. http://www.rockyhorrorwiki.org/wiki2/index.php?title=Ode_Records

19. http://www.onamrecords.com/Ode_Records.html

1. 20. http://www.rockymusic.org/about.php

20. Jewish Journal - Tom Teicholz., November 28, 2013

21. ibid

22. The Telegraph, Helen Brown, March 7, 2016

23. Taken from the booklet accompanying "Where There's Smoke There's Cheech & Chong " the 2002 anthology album)

24. https://www.latimes.com/entertainment/music/la-ca-ms-sunset-lou-adler-20170825-htmlstory.html

25. ibid

26. ibid

27. https://www.goodreads.com/book/show/3167357-forever

28. https://www.google.com/books/edition/Being_Hal_Ashby/ayGllCMwYD0C?hl=en&gbpv=1&dq=hal+ashby+mildred+cram+forever+movie&pg=PA177&printsec=frontcover

29. to author 7/2/20

30. https://catalog.afi.com/Catalog/moviedetails/56239

31. https://variety.com/2005/film/markets-festivals/chong-eisner-didn-t-light-up-over-smoke-1117917898/

32. "Shock Treatment" reviewed by Siskel and Ebert (Sneak Previews, 1981

33. https://www.scpr.org/programs/offramp/2010/09/11/16044/lou-adlers-one-failure-the-fabulous-stains/

34. https://www.ifc.com/2008/09/lou-adler-on-ladies-and-gentle)

35. https://www.wbur.org/npr/717757017/the-story-of-the-fabulous-stains-and-riot-grrrl

36. https://www.scpr.org/programs/offramp/2010/09/11/16044/lou-adlers-one-failure-the-fabulous-stains/

37. https://www.backstage.com/magazine/article/kenny-ortega-assembling-new-rocky-horror-cast-5454

38. https://deadline.com/2016/08/tim-curry-rocky-horror-picture-show-laverne-cox-tca-1201800009

39. https://www.nytimes.com/2016/10/20/arts/television/review-rocky-horror-remake-fox.htm

40. https://www.playbill.com/article/overnight-ratings-for-fox-tv-rocky-horror-disappointing

Chapter 17
Epilog

The room for growth of the "Rocky Horror" experience is huge. Passing fifty years is an achievement, but one that has come mainly from the United States market. The rest of the world could be open to the message "don't dream it, be it", a sentiment that has propelled the success of "Rocky Horror". This message is relevant everywhere. American pop culture, too, has no boundaries.

A famous forward-leaning media theory laid out in the 1960's by philosopher Marshall McLuhan was that humankind would become a collective identity, with a "tribal base". He called it the "Global Village". The "Rocky Horror" fans may be seen as a "tribal base" and their "global village" and the world connected through cyberspace using the internet, creating a community without borders.

How to recognize and nurture a global fan base will take stewardship and creativity. The logical participants include the several Adlers, who have so much skin in the "Rocky Horror" game. It's a great opportunity for the next generation to aim for a 75th Anniversary twenty-five years from now.

The End

www.ingramcontent.com/pod-product-compliance
Lightning Source LLC
Chambersburg PA
CBHW021718120626
46545CB00004B/1613